A Short Guide to Shakespeare

A Short Guide to
SHAKESPEARE

Sylvan Barnet

HBJ

A Harvest/HBJ Book
Harcourt Brace Jovanovich, Publishers
San Diego   New York   London

Library of Congress Cataloging in Publication Data

Barnet, Sylvan.
A short guide to Shakespeare.

(An Original harvest book HB 268)
The author's rev. and enl. introduction to
The complete Signet classic Shakespeare.
1. Shakespeare, William, 1564–1616. I. Title.
PR2976.B33 1974   822.3'3   73–13359
ISBN 0–15–681800–0

Printed in the United States of America

A B C D E F G H I J

Preface

When the forty paperback volumes of the Signet Shakespeare were collected into one hard-cover volume, I wrote a long introduction for the new edition. The present small book is that introduction, with the omission of some material not of general interest (a discussion of principles of editing, for example) and with the addition of some new material that may interest the general reader, such as discussions of modern staging and of film versions of Shakespeare. I have also amplified some of the comments on the plays, but a projected essay on reading the plays was abandoned because it only added up to advice to (1) keep a bookmark at the list of dramatis personae; (2) read slowly, unafraid even to move your lips; (3) try to be, in Henry James' words, one of the people on whom nothing is lost; but (4) do not be embarrassed if you occasionally cannot understand passages, for there are passages that no one yet has understood.

It is presumptuous to assume that anyone will read this book straight through, and therefore it may not be presumptuous to suggest that although the first half of the book tries to provide a background or context for the plays, the reader who wishes only to dip into the book briefly—perhaps in conjunction with reading or seeing a particular play—may find it useful to begin with the section "Style and Structure" and then proceed to the discussion of the play in question. I hope, of course, that readers will want to browse further, perhaps in the introductory remarks to the genre of the play studied and then in the additional background material in the first half of this *Short Guide*.

There remains the pleasant task of thanking my silent collaborators. Victor Weybright initiated the original paperback series; Ronald Campbell initiated the collected edition; John Ferrone saw this essay as suitable for a Harvest book; Richard Hosley provided valuable information about the Elizabethan playhouse; Morton Berman and William Burto improved the manuscript. It would take many pages to record the names of the critics who have helped to shape my ideas about Shakespeare; I can only say that I am grateful to all who have helped me to treasure the works of Shakespeare. The final debt, of course, is to Shakespeare. The man remains mysterious, but surely all readers sense a quality that his contemporaries remarked on, his "gentleness," and we remember words he gave to Orlando, "Let gentleness my strong enforcement be."

Contents

Contents

Contents

Part One

THE WRITER
AND HIS WORLD

1

Shakespeare's Life

Perhaps it is well to say at the outset that there is a good deal of evidence supporting the idea that William Shakespeare of Stratford and London wrote Shakespeare's plays. Several dozen other names have been put forward, the most notable of which are Bacon, Raleigh, Marlowe, and Queen Elizabeth; among the most amusing candidates are a nun named Anne Whately and an alleged illegitimate son of Queen Elizabeth. But there is no evidence to support any of these claims, all of which begin with the assumption that "the Stratford poacher" or "the Stratford butcher-boy" simply could not have written great plays and poems. A suitably learnèd or aristocratic candidate must then be found, and if the candidate has written under his own name, verbal echoes between the plays and the candidate's undisputed works must be collected. Sometimes ciphers are detected; for example, in the comically long word *honorifica-bilitudinitatibus* in *Love's Labor's Lost* (V.1.42), Bacon is said to have planted a Latin anagram, *Hi ludi F. Bacon nati tuiti orbi* ("These plays, offspring of F. Bacon, are preserved for the world"). A similar long word, *honorificabilitudine,* appears in a manuscript that contains some of Bacon's essays, but slight variations of this word appear elsewhere too; indeed, the word in the exact form in which it is found in *Love's Labor's Lost* had appeared in print a century before the birth of either Shakespeare or Bacon. Moreover, other anagrams can be extracted from it—for example, *Ubi Italicus ibi Danti honor fit* ("Where there is an Italian, there honor is paid to Dante"). Against all anti-Stratfordian theories stands the fact that scores of Elizabethans spoke of Shakespeare as a playwright, and no Elizabethan is on record as having believed that Shakespeare did not write the plays. If the actor William Shakespeare was a mere front for another author, how was the secret kept so well? Why, for example, was it never detected by Ben Jonson, who both in print and in conversation spoke of William Shakespeare's plays? (One answer that has been offered is that Jonson called Shakespeare the playwright because Jonson himself was the author of the plays but wished to hide his identity.) In short, if Shakespeare did not write the plays, a great many people were fooled during the thirty-five or so years between the date of the earliest plays and the publication in 1623 of the collected plays. Did the actors—some of whom worked with Shakespeare for about twenty years—never suspect that their dull colleague could not have written the plays he was passing off as his own? Or if, as another approach holds, so many people were not fooled but rather were in on the secret, how is it possible that in its own day this widely shared secret never leaked out? According to another desperate theory, which recognizes that the plays were regularly attributed to William Shakespeare but refuses to tolerate the idea of the Stratford poacher as an author, the plays were written not by William Shakespeare of Stratford but by another man of the same name. But to the charge that William Shakespeare of Stratford-upon-Avon was not William Shakespeare the actor and playwright there are many replies, at least two of which are simple and compelling: Jonson and others speak of the playwright as the "swan of Avon"; and in the Stratford man's will bequests are made to three actors in the London theatrical company who acted Shakespeare's plays, thus indisputably linking the Stratford man with the London theater. Not until 1769 was any doubt expressed about the authorship of the body of work ascribed to Shakespeare, and this doubt was founded on the *a priori* assumption that the plays must have been written by a learnèd man.

It seems reasonable, then, to believe what so many Elizabethans believed, that William Shakespeare of Stratford and London wrote the works of William Shakespeare.

Between the record of his baptism in Stratford on April 26, 1564, and the record of his burial in Stratford on April 25, 1616, many documents name Shakespeare, and many others name his parents, his children, and his grandchildren. On the whole these documents are official records of baptism, marriage, real-estate transactions, lawsuits, taxation, and death. Had Shakespeare, like Marlowe, been accused of atheism and been killed in a tavern brawl, or had he, like Jonson, killed a man, we would probably know more about him. Nonetheless, more facts are known about William Shakespeare than about any other playwright of the period except Ben Jonson. The facts should, however, be distinguished from the legends. The latter, inevitably more engaging and better known, tell us that the Stratford boy killed a calf in high style, poached deer and rabbits, and was forced to flee to London, where he held horses outside a playhouse. These legends are simply that; they may be true, but no evidence supports them, and it is well to stick to the facts—though inevitably the following account will include probabilities and conjectures as well.

Mary Arden, the dramatist's mother, was the daughter of a substantial landowner; about 1557 she married John Shakespeare, a glovemaker and trader in various farm commodities in the prosperous town of Stratford, which served as one of the market centers for farmers of the nearby villages in the county of Warwickshire. At this time Stratford had about two hundred families, probably adding up to something between one thousand and two thousand people. London had perhaps two hundred thousand or two hundred and fifty thousand people; probably only half a dozen other cities in England had as many as ten thousand. In 1557 John Shakespeare was a member of the Council (the governing body of Stratford), in 1558 a constable of the borough, in 1561 one of the two town chamberlains, in 1565 an alderman (entitling him to the appellation "Mr."), and in 1568 a high bailiff—the town's highest political office, equivalent to mayor. After 1577 John Shakespeare dropped out of local politics, perhaps because—as records of lawsuits and of property transactions suggest—he was in financial difficulties.

The birthday of William Shakespeare, the eldest son of this locally prominent man, is unrecorded; but the Stratford parish register indicates that the infant was baptized on April 26, 1564. (It is quite possible that he was born on April 23, as tradition holds, but this date has probably been assigned for three reasons: some infants were baptized when they were three days old; fifty-two years later Shakespeare died on April 23; and April 23 is the day of England's patron saint, Saint George.)

In Elizabethan England when a child was four or five years old he attended a petty (elementary) school, where he learned to memorize some prayers and passages from the Scripture and learned to write English; in the third year he began Latin. Most girls completed their formal education at seven or eight, but boys, unless their families were very poor and needed the child's labor, generally went on to the grammar school, where they remained until they were fourteen or fifteen. The school year was longer than it is today: the school week was six days long, and the school day about eight or ten hours. The Elizabethan curriculum only rarely included mathematics, and it regularly ignored the natural sciences and modern languages, but it taught a good deal of Latin grammar, rhetoric, logic, and Roman literature. Among the authors studied in the Elizabethan grammar school were Cicero, Plautus, Terence, Virgil, and Ovid, all of whom left their marks on Shakespeare's plays.

The attendance records of the Stratford grammar school of the period are not extant, but it is reasonable to assume that the son of a local official attended the school and received substantial training in Latin. The comic scene in *The Merry Wives of Windsor* (IV.i), in which a schoolmaster asks a pupil named William to exhibit his competence in Latin, should not lead us to think that the masters were ill-trained; the two masters of the Stratford grammar school from Shakespeare's seventh to fifteenth years held Oxford degrees. Thus the late seventeenth-century report that Shakespeare "understood Latin pretty well" is entirely credible. It is not irreconcilable with Ben Jonson's statement that Shakespeare had "small Latin and less Greek," for Jonson was an immensely learnèd poet who would inevitably have regarded anything less than expertness as "small." Whether Shakespeare knew any foreign language other than Latin—Jonson's reference to his Greek is probably as generous as his reference to his Latin is niggardly—is uncertain. A few of the sources for Shakespeare's plays exist today only in Italian, but possibly there were lost English versions; in any case, Shakespeare's knowledge of Latin would have enabled him to get the gist of an Italian story. Of his knowledge of French, a little more can be said: in *Henry V* there is an entire scene (an English lesson) in French, so it seems reasonable to assume that Shakespeare had at least a working knowledge of the language.

During Shakespeare's childhood there are several records of his father's dealings but none of the boy's doings. After the registration of his baptism, the next records that name Shakespeare are documents of November 27 and 28, 1582, recording the issuance of a marriage license to "William Shagspere . . . and Anne Hathwey." Anne Hathaway, who was eight years her husband's senior, bore a child in May 1583. Perhaps the marriage was necessary, but perhaps the couple had earlier engaged in a formal "troth plight," which would have rendered their children legitimate even if no further ceremony had been performed. In 1585 Anne Hathaway bore Shakespeare twins.

That Shakespeare was born is excellent; that he married and had children is pleasant; but that we know nothing about his departure from Stratford to London, or about the beginning of his theatrical career, is lamentable and must be admitted. We would gladly sacrifice details about his children's baptism for details about his earliest days on the stage. Perhaps the poaching episode is true (but it is first reported almost a century after Shakespeare's death), or perhaps he first left Stratford to be a schoolteacher, as another theory holds. Perhaps he was moved by

> Such wind as scatters young men through the world,
> To seek their fortunes farther than at home,
> Where small experience grows.
>
> (*The Taming of the Shrew,* I.ii.49–51)

There are no existing records of Shakespeare's activities between 1585 and 1592. One can with safety say only that at some time prior to 1592 he went to London and commenced his theatrical career. In 1592, thanks to the cantankerousness of Robert Greene, a rival playwright and a pamphleteer, the first reference—a snarling one—to Shakespeare as an actor and playwright appears. Greene warns those of his own educated friends who wrote for the theater against actors—"puppets . . . that spake from our mouths"—and particularly against one actor who had presumed to turn playwright:

There is an upstart crow, beautified with our feathers, that with his *tiger's heart wrapped in a player's hide* supposes he is as well able to bombast out a blank verse as the best of you, and being an absolute Johannes-factotum is in his own conceit the only Shake-scene in a country.

The reference to the player, as well as the allusion to a crow (which in a fable strutted in borrowed plumage, as an actor struts in fine words not his own), makes it clear that by this date Shakespeare had both acted and written. Possibly there is a charge of plagiarism here too, for the crow was sometimes used to symbolize a writer who pilfered from others. That Shakespeare is meant is indicated not only by "Shake-scene" but by the parody of a line from one of Shakespeare's plays, *3 Henry VI:* "O, tiger's heart wrapped in a woman's hide." If Shakespeare was prominent enough by 1592 to be attacked by an envious dramatist, he probably had served an apprenticeship in the theater for at least a few years. If Greene's allusion to the crow does imply plagiarism, quite possibly Shakespeare began his career as a dramatist by revising earlier plays. Certainly he was to do this later on a grand scale, in *Hamlet* and *King Lear,* for instance.

Numerous subsequent references to Shakespeare indicate that as early as 1594 he was not only an actor but also a partner in a new theatrical company, the Lord Chamberlain's Men, which soon became one of London's two chief companies. Acting was not considered a suitable profession for a gentleman, and it occasionally drew the scorn of university men, who resented writing speeches for persons less educated than themselves. But acting was respectable enough: prosperous players were in effect members of the bourgeoisie, and there is nothing to suggest that Stratford considered William Shakespeare less than a solid citizen. In 1596 the Shakespeares were granted a coat of arms. The grant was made to Shakespeare's father, who as bailiff had been (in the words of an appended note) "the queen's officer," but one can conjecture that William Shakespeare—who the next year bought the second-largest house in town—had arranged the matter on his own behalf. In subsequent transactions he is usually styled a gentleman. (The title cannot mean anything to us, and yet in its modern sense it is singularly applicable; for all their forcefulness, his works are conspicuously gentle, captivating us by their decency.) The house he bought in 1597 was built by a man who later became Lord Mayor of London; in 1643 it was still fine enough for Queen Henrietta Maria to spend two nights there as the guest of Shakespeare's daughter and granddaughter. Records of purchases and investments in later years demonstrate both Shakespeare's prosperity and his involvement with Stratford even during his theatrical career in London.

In 1593 and 1594 Shakespeare published *Venus and Adonis* and *The Rape of Lucrece*, two narrative poems dedicated to Henry Wriothesley, Earl of Southampton, and he may well have written most or all of his sonnets in the nineties. But Shakespeare's major literary activity during this time was devoted to the theater. (It may be significant that the two narrative poems were written between the summer of 1592 and the spring of 1594, in years when the plague closed the theaters.) In 1594, as has been mentioned, he was a member of a theatrical company called the Lord Chamberlain's Men (which in 1603 changed its name to the King's Men); until he retired to Stratford (about 1611, apparently), he was with this remarkably stable company. From 1599 the company acted primarily at the Globe Theatre, in which Shakespeare held a one-tenth interest. Of the more than three hundred known Renaissance English playwrights, some of whom acted as well as wrote, only

Shakespeare is known to have been entitled to a share in the profits of the playhouse.

Shakespeare probably completed his first sixteen plays by the end of 1598—in a decade or less. In the next ten years he was almost as prolific, writing perhaps thirteen or fourteen plays, including many that are his greatest. In the remaining years of his career Shakespeare seems to have slowed down a bit, writing about a play a year. Some evidence suggests that he gradually withdrew from the theater to live in Stratford. From his acting and playwriting and his share in the Globe Theatre, Shakespeare made a considerable amount of money. He put it to work, making substantial investments in Stratford real estate, although during his career he lived in London. By 1612, when a document of a London court identifies him as "William Shakespeare of Stratford-upon-Avon," he was apparently again living in Stratford. When he revised his will in 1616 (less than a month before he died), following the usual practice he sought to leave most of his property intact to his descendants: first to his daughter, Susanna, then to her eldest surviving son, and so on. But all four of his grandchildren died without lineal heirs, and the estate was eventually broken up. Of the small bequests made to relatives and friends (including three actors, Richard Burbage, John Heminges, and Henry Condell), the bequest to his wife of the second-best bed has provoked the most comment; perhaps it was the bed the couple had slept in, the best bed having been reserved for visitors. In any case, had Shakespeare not excepted it, the bed would have gone along with the rest of his household possessions to his daughter and her husband. Nor need we fret that Shakespeare's wife was left with only a bed. The laws of the period assured a widow of one third of the income from her husband's estate during her lifetime.

The cause of Shakespeare's death is not known, but a clergyman who settled in Stratford in 1662—almost fifty years after Shakespeare's death—recorded in his diary that "Shakespeare, Drayton, and Ben Jonson had a merry meeting, and it seems drank too hard, for Shakespeare died of a fever there contracted." This may or may not be true. In any case, on April

25, 1616, Shakespeare was buried under the floor of the chancel in the church at Stratford. An unattractive monument to his memory, placed on a wall near the grave, says he died on April 23. Carved on the slab over the grave itself are the lines, perhaps written by Shakespeare himself, that (more than his literary fame) have kept his bones undisturbed in the crowded burial ground beneath the church floor, where old bones were often dislodged to make way for new:

> Good friend, for Jesus' sake forbear
> To dig the dust enclosèd here.
> Blessed be the man that spares these stones
> And cursed be he that moves my bones.

2
The Canon

Thirty-seven plays, one hundred fifty-four sonnets, two long nondramatic poems, and one short elegy constitute the Shakespeare canon, or list of accepted works. A thirty-eighth play, *The Two Noble Kinsmen,* has increasingly gained acceptance as having been written at least in part by Shakespeare. One other play in the apocrypha, or body of writing sometimes attributed to Shakespeare but not widely accepted as authentic, deserves mention. This is *Sir Thomas More,* which survives in manuscript and which includes three pages that some experts believe are in Shakespeare's handwriting. Possibly, too, some of Shakespeare's plays are lost, but probably the canon preserves all or almost all of his work.

The dates of composition of most of the works are highly uncertain, but there is often evidence of a *terminus a quo* (starting point) and/or a *terminus ad quem* (ending point) that provides a framework for intelligent guessing. For example, *Richard II* cannot have been written earlier than 1595, the publication date of some material to which it is indebted; *The Merchant of Venice* cannot have been written later than 1598, the year Francis Meres mentioned it. Dates are often attributed to plays on the basis of style, and although conjectures about style usually rest on other conjectures, sooner or later one must rely on one's literary sense. There is no real proof, for example, that *Othello* was not written as early as *Julius Caesar,* but one feels that *Othello* is a later play, and because the first record of its performance is 1604, one is glad enough to set its composition at that date or a little earlier and not push it back into Shakespeare's early years. The following chronology, then, is as much indebted to informed guesswork and literary sensitivity as it is to fact. The dates, necessarily imprecise, indicate what is essentially a scholarly consensus. The dates of the earliest plays are especially uncertain because it is not known when Shakespeare began writing for the stage (that his first plays were not written earlier than 1588 is only a conjecture) and because some of them show signs of having been revised several years after they were written. *Love's Labor's Lost* especially suggests an early date, perhaps 1588, and a revision in 1595 or so.

PLAYS

1588–93	*The Comedy of Errors*
1588–92	*2 Henry VI*
1588–92	*3 Henry VI*
1588–92	*1 Henry VI*
1592–93	*Richard III*
1592–94	*Titus Andronicus*
1593–94	*The Taming of the Shrew*
1593–94	*The Two Gentlemen of Verona*
1588–95	*Love's Labor's Lost*
1594–96	*Romeo and Juliet*
1595	*Richard II*
1594–96	*A Midsummer Night's Dream*
1590–97	*King John*
1596–97	*The Merchant of Venice*
1597	*1 Henry IV*
1597–98	*2 Henry IV*
1598–1600	*Much Ado About Nothing*
1598–99	*Henry V*
1599	*Julius Caesar*
1599–1600	*As You Like It*
1600–02	*Twelfth Night*
1600–01	*Hamlet*
1597–1601	*The Merry Wives of Windsor*
1601–02	*Troilus and Cressida*

A Short Guide to Shakespeare

1602–04	*All's Well That Ends Well*
1603–04	*Othello*
1604	*Measure for Measure*
1604–09	*Timon of Athens*
1605–06	*King Lear*
1605–06	*Macbeth*
1606–07	*Antony and Cleopatra*
1607–09	*Coriolanus*
1608–09	*Pericles*
1609–10	*Cymbeline*
1610–11	*The Winter's Tale*
1611	*The Tempest*
1612–13	*Henry VIII*
1613	*The Two Noble Kinsmen*

POEMS

1592	*Venus and Adonis*
1593–94	*The Rape of Lucrece*
1593–1600	*Sonnets*
1600–01	*The Phoenix and the Turtle*

3

The Theaters and Actors

A good deal of theatrical activity took place in England during Shakespeare's youth, but much of it was not performed by professionals in a theater. There was play-acting in the schools and universities; there was pageantry in the streets; there were masques at court. This section, however, is concerned only with the professional theater. (For a discussion of some of the amateur traditions behind Elizabethan drama, see pp. 30–38.)

THE THEATERS

In Shakespeare's infancy, Elizabethan actors performed wherever they could—possibly in bearbaiting and bullbaiting arenas, and certainly in the courtyards of inns, in great halls, and at court. The innyards probably made rather unsatisfactory theaters; on some days they were unavailable because carters bringing goods to London used them as depots; when available, they had to be rented from the innkeeper. Perhaps most important, London inns were under the jurisdiction of the Common Council of London, which was not well disposed toward theatricals. In 1574 the Common Council required that plays and playing places in London be licensed. It asserted that

sundry great disorders and inconveniences have been found to ensue to this city by the inordinate haunting of great multitudes of people, specially youth, to plays, interludes, and shows, namely occasion of frays and quarrels, evil practices of incontinency in great inns having chambers and secret places adjoining to their open stages and galleries,

and ordered that innkeepers who wished licenses to hold performances put up a bond and make contributions to the poor. The requirement that plays and innyard theaters be licensed, along with the other drawbacks of playing at inns, probably drove James Burbage, a carpenter turned actor, to rent in 1576 a plot of land northeast of the city walls and to build there, on property outside the jurisdiction of the city, England's first permanent construction designed for plays. He called it simply the Theatre. About all that is known of its construction is that it was made of wood and was in the shape of an "amphitheatrum," that is, round or approximately so, like a bearbaiting arena. Presumably Burbage erected a stage in the yard, and behind the stage a dressing room from which actors could enter the stage through doorways that were perhaps fitted with hanging cloths. Such an arrangement probably resembled the curtained booths at the rear of the temporary stages that players used in the market theaters or the hall-screen in a great house that masked the doors to the pantry, kitchen, and buttery from the hall itself but allowed entrance to the hall through doorways in the hall-screen. The Theatre was probably three stories high, and the yard was partly sheltered with a roof topped by a hut, which housed suspension gear for flying effects. Burbage's Theatre soon had imitators, the most famous of which was the Globe (1599), built by Shakespeare and his fellow sharers in the Lord Chamberlain's company. The Globe was built on the Bankside, south of the Thames (again outside the city's jurisdiction), and was made from timbers of the Theatre, which had been dismantled and transported across London when Burbage's lease ran out.

There are three important sources of information about the structure of Elizabethan playhouses: drawings, a contract, and stage directions in plays. Of drawings, only the so-called De Witt drawing (about 1596) of the Swan—actually a friend's copy of De Witt's drawing—is of much significance. Although the De Witt drawing raises several questions, it gives us a good deal of information about the Elizabethan theater. It shows a

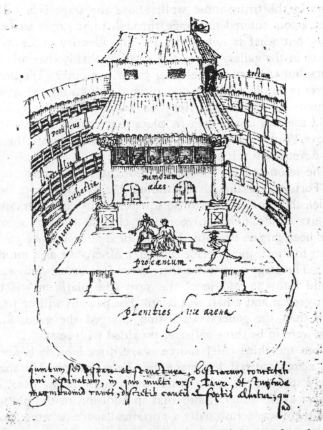

*Arend Van Buchel's copy of Johannes De Witt's now lost drawing
of the Swan, showing the theater as De Witt saw it in 1596.*
(University Library, Utrecht, Ms. 842, fol. 132r.)

circular building of three galleries, with a stage jutting from a
wall into the yard formed by the surrounding galleries. The
galleries are roofed, and part of the stage is covered by a roof
that projects from the rear and is supported at its front by two
posts. The groundlings, who paid a penny to stand in front of
the stage or at its sides, were exposed to the sky. (Performances
in such a playhouse were held only in the daytime; artificial
illumination was not used.) At the rear of the stage are two

doors in the tiring-house wall; above the stage is a gallery. That actors entered the stage through these doors seems obvious, but what is not obvious is the identity of De Witt's figures in the gallery above the stage. Probably they are spectators, but why are all the other galleries empty? (The neatest answer is that it would be difficult and tedious for the artist to populate all of the galleries.) As will be seen below, actors could use this upper area in plays that required them to be "above," but when plays did not require such action, the area was devoted entirely to spectators.

The second major source of information, the contract for the Fortune, specifies that although the Globe was to be its model, the Fortune was to be square, eighty feet outside and fifty-five inside. (The polygonal or circular theaters seem to have been larger: perhaps the interior diameter was eighty or eighty-five feet, the exterior diameter ninety-five or a hundred feet.) The stage was to be forty-three feet broad and was to extend into the middle of the yard (the platform was thus twenty-seven and a half feet deep). For patrons willing to pay more than the general admission charged the groundlings, there were to be three galleries provided with seats.

From the third chief source, stage directions, it is known that actors entered the stage by doors, presumably spaced widely apart at the rear (*"Enter one citizen at one door, and another at the other"*), and that in addition to the platform stage there was occasionally a curtained space (whether booth or alcove) at the rear of the platform that allowed for "discovery" scenes and a playing space "aloft" or "above" used to represent such areas as the top of a city's walls or the window of a room above the street. Doubtless each theater had its own peculiarities; but it is possible to talk about a "typical" Elizabethan theater if we bear in mind that no theater need exactly have fitted the description, just as no father is a typical father with 3.7 children. This hypothetical Elizabethan theater is wooden, round or polygonal (in *Henry V* Shakespeare calls it a "wooden O"), and capable of holding about three thousand spectators—perhaps two thousand standing in the yard around the projecting elevated stage and one thousand seated in the three roofed galleries. Because the spectators stood rather than sat in chairs on the ground level, and because the three galleries circled the auditorium rather than being confined to the rear (as in most proscenium-arch theaters), a large number of people could be squeezed into a relatively small building. This means that Shakespeare had a stage that afforded remarkable intimacy between actors and audience, a stage on which, for example, Hamlet's soliloquies would not have to be delivered as "big" speeches. The stage, protected by a roof called the "cover" or "heavens," was entered by two doors. These doors may have been curtained (although curtains are not shown in the De Witt drawing of the Swan) and thus may have served as the area for "discoveries" mentioned above. Or there may have been a third opening, a curtained booth or alcove against the rear wall between these two doors. In *The Merchant of Venice,* for example, "the curtain" is opened three times to reveal Portia's three caskets. In *1 Henry IV* Falstaff hides and is later discovered *"behind the arras."* But a door itself, without a curtain, would presumably have served as an entrance to Juliet's tomb. When Romeo *"opens the tomb,"* he probably opened a pair of double-hung doors, like those in the De Witt drawing, to reveal Juliet lying on a coffin. Surprisingly, such discovery scenes are very rare in Elizabethan drama. It is worth mentioning that usually no more than two persons are discovered at once, which suggests that the area was too small to be considered (as it sometimes is in the twentieth century) an "inner stage." After being discovered, the character or characters did not move about in the discovery space; they walked out onto the stage. Behind the stage was the "tiring house" (attiring house, or dressing room), and above the doors was a gallery that sometimes held spectators but that was also used, for example, as the bedroom window from which Romeo—according to a stage direction in one text—*"goeth down"* or as the castle wall from which young Arthur in *King John* leaps down. Some evidence suggests that a throne was lowered onto the platform stage, perhaps from the stage cover; certainly characters descended from the stage through a trap or traps into the cellar, or "hell."

Sometimes this space beneath the platform was used to accommodate a sound-effects man or musician (in *Antony and Cleopatra* "*music of the hautboys is under the stage*") or an actor (in *Hamlet* the "*Ghost cries under the stage*"). Most characters simply walked on and off, but because there was no curtain at the front of the stage, corpses had to be carried off—thus an Elizabethan Hamlet had to lug Polonius' body into the adjoining room.

Such may have been the so-called public theater. There was also another kind of theater, called the "private theater" because its much greater admission charge limited its audience to the rich or the prodigal. This type of theater was basically a large room, entirely roofed and therefore artificially illuminated, with a stage at one end and a tiring house behind the stage. In 1576, a year before the first permanent public theater was built, such a theater was established in Blackfriars, a Dominican priory in London that had been suppressed in 1538 and confiscated by the crown and thus was not under the city's jurisdiction. All the actors in the Blackfriars theater were boys about eight to thirteen years old. This private theater had a precarious existence and ceased operations in 1584. In 1596 James Burbage, who had already made theatrical history by building the Theatre, began to construct a second Blackfriars theater. He died in 1597, and for several years this second Blackfriars theater was used by a troupe of boys. But in 1608 two of Burbage's sons and five other actors (including Shakespeare) became joint operators of the theater, using it in the winter, when the open-air Globe was unsuitable. Perhaps such a smaller theater (its capacity was about seven hundred), roofed, artificially illuminated, and patronized by a fashionable audience, exerted an influence on Shakespeare's later plays, but it would be a mistake to think either that these later plays have fundamentally different staging needs or that they are essentially different in spirit from Shakespeare's earlier work. It should be noted, too, that Elizabethan theatrical companies were occasionally called upon to give a performance at court, on a temporary stage in a room illuminated by candles and torches. But since a play thus staged was commonly selected from the company's repertory by the queen's Master of the Revels, a performance at court was probably not vastly different from a performance in a theater.

Performances in the private theaters may well have had intermissions, during which music was played, but in the public theaters the action was probably uninterrupted, flowing from scene to scene almost without a break. Actors entered, spoke, and exited, and other actors immediately entered and established a new locale (if necessary) by a few properties and by words and gestures. Here are some samples of how Shakespeare set the place or the time of his plays:

> JULIET
> Wilt thou be gone? It is not yet near day.
> It was the nightingale, and not the lark,
> That pierced the fearful hollow of thine ear.
>
> ROMEO
> It was the lark, the herald of the morn;
> No nightingale. Look, love, what envious streaks
> Do lace the severing clouds in yonder East.
>   (*Romeo and Juliet,* III.v.1–3,6–8)

Sometimes the setting of locale is more direct:

> DUNCAN
> This castle hath a pleasant seat; the air
> Nimbly and sweetly recommends itself
> Unto our gentle senses.   (*Macbeth,* I.vi.1–3)
>
> CAPTAIN
> This is Illyria, lady.   (*Twelfth Night,* I.ii.2)
>
> ROSALIND
> Well, this is the Forest of Arden.   (*As You Like It,* II.iv.14)

But it is a mistake to conceive of the Elizabethan stage as bare. Although the Chorus in *Henry V* calls the stage an "unworthy scaffold" and urges the spectators to "eke out our performance with your mind," the stage façade itself was apparently richly decorated, and the underside of the cover was adorned with stars. Moreover, considerable spectacle took place on the platform stage itself, which could accommodate thrones, altars, and chariots, as well as colorful processions. In the last act of *Macbeth,* for example, five stage directions call for *"drum and colors,"* and another sort of appeal to the eye is made by the stage direction *"Enter Macduff, with Macbeth's head."*

THE ACTORS

In the late Middle Ages religious plays were performed by members of various craft guilds: bakers, butchers, goldsmiths, and so on acted in plays on biblical subjects. Amateur theatrical activity flourished (we should also keep in mind Robin Hood plays, Saint George plays, May games, and other amateur seasonal theatricals of a folkloric nature), creating a climate in which professionalism could develop. By the middle of the fifteenth century traveling troupes were staging plays throughout England. These troupes were small—usually consisting of four actors—but they must have been highly skilled, for their livelihood depended on doing better what innumerable amateurs were also doing. By the middle of the sixteenth century some traveling troupes included as many as a dozen actors, with boys playing the female roles. In their social origins these actors were generally men like Bottom the weaver and his fellows who in *A Midsummer Night's Dream* perform a play before the duke. But the ineptitude of Bottom's amateur company should not be confused with the skill of the professionals; the craftsmen who left their looms or cobbler's benches to become professional actors had to be expert in their new craft if they were to survive.

For various reasons, including the break-up of feudal households during the Wars of the Roses and the dissolution of the monasteries, Tudor England had a large number of unemployed wanderers, and laws were devised to restrain them. Because a "masterless man" was considered unnatural—the more so because there was a labor shortage—traveling actors were nominally considered the "servants" of a nobleman; but from this patron they usually got only a license or patent and payment for an occasional performance in his household on a festive day. The actors depended for their livelihood on the patronage of the general public, and the license was necessary if they were to reach that public. When Shakespeare's company received the patronage of King James I in 1603, its license read as follows:

Know ye that We of our special grace, certain knowledge, and mere motion have licensed and authorized and by these presents do license and authorize these our servants Lawrence Fletcher, William Shakespeare, Richard Burbage, Augustine Phillips, John Heminges, Henry Condell, William Sly, Robert Armin, Richard Cowley, and the rest of their associates freely to use and exercise the art and faculty of playing comedies, tragedies, histories, interludes, moralities, pastorals, stage plays, and such others like as they have already studied or hereafter shall use or study, as well for the recreation of our loving subjects as for our solace and pleasure when we shall think good to see them, during our pleasure. And the said comedies, tragedies, histories, interludes, moralities, pastorals, stage plays, and such like to show and exercise publicly to their best commodity, when the infection of the plague shall decrease, as well within their now usual house called the Globe within our county of Surrey, as also within any town halls or moot halls or other convenient places within the liberties and freedom of any other city, university, town, or borough whatsoever within our said realms and dominions. Willing and commanding you and every of you, as you tender our pleasure, not only to permit and suffer them herein without any your hindrances or molestations during our said pleasure, but also to be aiding and assisting to them, if any wrong be to them offered. And to allow them such former courtesies as hath been given to men of their place and quality, and also that further favor you shall show to these our servants for our sake we shall take kindly at your hands.

Doubtless a most useful document.

By the end of the sixteenth century, despite harassment by puritanical forces, the status of actors was fairly secure: acting was recognized as a "trade" or "profession," subject not to local authorities but to the crown through the Master of the Revels and his superior, the Lord Chamberlain. Therefore, although the Revels Office censored plays and could be a powerful enemy when it suspected that a play harbored seditious ideas, it was for the most part (like the lords who lent acting companies their nominal patronage) an important ally of the players: it arranged for occasional remunerative performances at court, and more important, it stood between the players and the local bourgeois officials, who often regarded theatrical performances as a waste of time, or as indecent shows, or worst of all as vestiges of Roman Catholic activities. (It should be remembered that the old religious drama survived in some parts of England past the middle of the sixteenth century.) There is a large body of anti-theatrical writing, much of it amusing in its abusiveness, but one example, from a sermon written in 1578 by John Stockwood, should suffice:

Will not a filthy play, with the blast of a trumpet, sooner call thither a thousand than an hour's tolling of a bell bring to the sermon a hundred? . . . If you resort to the Theatre, the Curtain, and other places of plays in the city, you shall on the Lord's day have these places, with many other that I cannot reckon, so full as possibly they can throng.

Even allowing for the exaggeration of an indignant competitor, Stockwood's comments help to indicate the magnitude of theatrical activity that took place in the period of Shakespeare's youth.

A theatrical company such as the Lord Chamberlain's Men was a substantial business enterprise. The company was formed in the summer of 1594; if Shakespeare was not a charter member, he joined the company soon after its formation, for he is specified as a member in March 1595, and he stayed with it for the remainder of his professional life. The company's organization was rather medieval, consisting of three groups that resembled the craft-guild hierarchy of master craftsmen, journeymen, and apprentices: (1) senior actors, such as Shakespeare, called "fellows" or "sharers" because each owned a share in the plays and the properties, and therefore shared in the profits; (2) hired men, who performed minor roles or served as musicians, prompters, doorkeepers, and so on, and did not share in the profits; and (3) boys, who were in effect apprenticed to the sharers and played most or all of the female roles. (Possibly the garrulous old Nurse in *Romeo and Juliet* was played by a man rather than by a boy.) A boy entered the company when he was about ten, trained for a while, and then acted female roles until his voice changed or he grew too tall for the part. That all the performers were male should not seem strange; all the performers in classical Greek, Chinese, and Japanese drama also were male, as were the performers in the folk plays (see p. 30). It would seem that drama, when it is still close to ceremony and not yet fully dedicated to realism, prefers men to represent women. Shakespeare's company expanded over the years, beginning with five sharers and ending with twelve, but it probably never had more than about two dozen actors. Even *Henry VIII*, which has forty-one speaking parts, can be performed by about a dozen actors by doubling and tripling.

No evidence suggests that after 1594 Shakespeare ever wrote for a company other than the Lord Chamberlain's Men. Doubtless the composition of his company left its mark on his plays; Shakespeare knew what it could do, and he knew for whom he had to write parts. For example, because there were probably only two or three boys at any given time who could play important roles, and another two or three in training, Shakespeare's plays rarely have more than four significant female roles, though of course a larger number can be handled by doubling. The fact that so many of Shakespeare's heroines are motherless—for example, Rosalind and Celia in *As You Like It*—is probably due to the restrictions imposed by the company rather than to anything in Shakespeare's psychology. Probably, too, the availability of a good clown encouraged Shakespeare to write in a clown's part, and so on. Nothing in the sources of *King Lear* suggests a clown, and if Shakespeare decided to invent the part of a fool for the play because the noted comic actor Robert Armin was a member of the company, no one can regret Shakespeare's willingness to provide a part for him. (It might be argued with equal validity, of course, that the audience wanted a clown, and so the company made it its business to have one.) Viewed one way, Shakespeare was in bondage to his company; viewed another way, Shakespeare had the advantage of knowing what his actors could and could not do before he put pen to paper. And his own experience as an actor must have been an enormous asset to the playwright.

A company performed five or six times a week, giving in a season twenty-five or thirty different plays, about half of which were new in the repertory and the remainder either recent favorites or revivals of older plays. Occasionally a play was given two or three consecutive performances, but commonly the program changed every day, and the same play was rarely acted twice in one week. Thus in a month a company might perform a dozen different plays. Although no annual records for the Lord Chamberlain's Men are extant, it is possible to get an idea of its activities from the records of its rival, the Admiral's Men. Between 1594 and 1597 the Admiral's Men gave 728 performances of fifty-five plays; or to take a more microscopic view, between August 1595 and February 1596 it gave 150 performances of thirty different plays, fourteen of which were new.

Existing evidence on the style of Elizabethan acting is open to various interpretations. There are essentially two schools of thought: one sees Elizabethan acting as realistic (or natural); the other sees it as conventional (or formal). Advocates of the realistic theory point to various Elizabethan passages that praise actors as lifelike: Hamlet, for example, warns the players against ranting, and this is taken as evidence that the actors in *Hamlet* did not rant. But this very statement can also be taken as evidence that actors normally ranted, and that Shakespeare was trying to restrain his actors. Moreover, even if we agree that the actors in *Hamlet* did not rant, we need not conclude that they acted realistically. Another piece of evidence usually taken as indicating that acting was realistic is John Webster's comment on the ability of a good actor: "What we see him personate, we think truly done before us." But one can reply that every age insists that its good actors are natural. The acting in the motion pictures of the thirties, for example, seems quaint to us today, though it struck its contemporaries as thoroughly lifelike.

Those who argue that Elizabethan acting was formal rather than natural insist that the conditions of the stage required formal acting: performances were given in daylight, even though some scenes occurred at night; boys performed female parts; the language of the play was commonly poetry rather than daily speech. In addition, characters sometimes addressed the audience directly, breaking (it is argued) any illusion of the reality of the world on the stage. Such arguments in behalf of formal acting have much merit, yet they cannot be taken as proof that Elizabethan acting was *highly* stylized and devoid of naturalism. The dialogue in the plays themselves, for example, provides evidence that characters did not silently walk across the stage, take up a position, and then declaim; they spoke while they walked, while they dressed, and so on. Probably, then, it is safest to conclude that although natural acting was highly praised and unnatural acting ridiculed, the acting of Shakespeare's day was a combination of both styles, and it was probably somewhat more naturalistic than the acting of his youth, which had come to seem bombastic. In *A Midsummer Night's Dream* Bottom is perhaps old-fashioned when he says he "will move storms" and when he yearns for "a part to tear a cat in, to make all split." A few years later Hamlet deplores actors who split the ears of the groundlings.

Not much is known about the costumes that Elizabethan actors wore, but at least three points are clear: (1) many of the costumes were sumptuous versions of contemporary Elizabethan dress; (2) some attempts were made to approximate the dress of certain occupations and of antique or exotic characters such as Romans, Turks, and Jews; (3) some costumes indicated that the wearer was supernatural. Evidence for elaborate contemporary dress can be found in the many references to Elizabethan clothing (doublets, hose, and so on) in the plays themselves and in contemporary comments about the "sumptuous" players who wore the discarded clothing of noblemen, as well as in various account books that itemize such things as "a scarlet cloak with two broad gold laces, with gold buttons of the same down the sides." The attempt at approximating the dress of certain occupations and nationalities also can be documented from the plays themselves, and it derives additional confirmation from a drawing—the only extant picture of an identifiable Elizabethan stage production—of a scene from *Titus Andronicus.* The drawing, probably done in 1594

A drawing (circa 1594) of characters in Titus Andronicus, *showing the mixture of pseudo-Roman and contemporary costumes.*
(© the Marquess of Bath)

or 1595, shows Queen Tamora pleading for mercy. She wears a robe and a crown; Titus wears a toga and a wreath, but two soldiers behind him wear costumes fairly close to Elizabethan dress. There is, however, some conflicting evidence: in *Julius Caesar* a reference is made to Caesar's doublet, which, if taken literally, suggests that even the protagonist did not wear Roman clothing; and certainly the lesser characters, who are said to wear hats, did not wear Roman garb. But perhaps in its context the word *doublet* merely denotes a garment for the upper part of the body, not the specifically Elizabethan garment. The use of symbolic costumes for supernatural creatures is nicely illustrated by a property listed in the journal of an Elizabethan theatrical entrepreneur: "a robe for to go invisible." In *The Tempest* this stage direction appears: *"Enter Ariel, invisible"* (III.ii). Possibly this symbolic robe was worn; possibly the stage direction is merely an instruction to the actors, but certainly in III.iii, *"Enter Ariel, like a harpy,"* a symbolic costume was used. Finally, it should be mentioned that even ordinary clothing can be symbolic: Hamlet's "inky cloak," for example, sets him aside from the brightly dressed members of Claudius' court and symbolizes his mourning; the fresh clothes that are put on King Lear partly symbolize his return to sanity. This device, of course, is not confined to the tragedies. Near the end of *Much Ado About Nothing*, just before Claudio's bride is restored to him—giving him, in effect, a new life—Don Pedro says to Claudio, "Come, let us hence and put on other weeds." Claudio's reappearance, presumably in a new splendid costume, is a visual representation of his renewal.

4

The Dramatic Background

It has been mentioned that a good deal of theatrical and quasi-theatrical activity took place in England in Shakespeare's youth. It is not possible to discuss here such activities as jousts and tournaments, which were highly ritualized and spectacular encounters with conflict at their heart, and public executions, in which the condemned man was allowed to make a speech to the assembled crowd, but there is no doubt that such activities influenced Shakespeare's plays, as can be seen from the interrupted joust in *Richard II* (I.iii) and the report of the Thane of Cawdor's words just before he is executed in *Macbeth* (I.iv.1–11) or Othello's words just before he kills himself (V.ii.337–55). Rather, this section will be concerned with five sorts of drama, and the subsequent discussions of Shakespeare's comedies, histories, and tragedies will occasionally amplify some of the points raised here.

First, an enduring drama existed among the folk, the peasants and artisans who enacted annual playlets celebrating the renewal of the year, which had "died" in the winter and been "reborn" in the spring. Often these festive plays were transferred from the spring or summer to the Christmas festivities, for Christmas symbolized the possibility of the renewal or rebirth of fallen man. Commonly the players would visit their lord's manor house and perform their rudimentary playlet, thus in a way bringing into the household the spirit of rebirth and joy that was being enacted. The most famous of such traditional entertainments was the Saint George play, which dealt with a combat, a death, and a resurrection and concluded

with a blessing, or wish for prosperity. Here is the end of a version that was performed at Christmas:

> I am Father Christmas! Hold, men, hold!
> Be there loaf in your locker, and sheep in your fold,
> A fire on the hearth, and good luck for your lot,
> Money in your pocket, and a pudding in the pot!

As the discussion of Shakespeare's comedies will indicate, the
overall movement was from a troubled or deathlike state (for
example, at the beginning of *A Midsummer Night's Dream* if
Egeus' daughter will not obey her father, the law may sentence
her "to death, or to a vow of single life") to a state of prosperity, fertility, and joy, symbolized by a feast, a dance, or
especially, a marriage. Other festivities included May games,
especially the Whitsun pastorals, which Shakespeare alludes
to in *The Winter's Tale* (IV.iv). May Day activities involved the
choice of a Queen of the May or of a Maid Marian; the Queen
was given a garland and then entertained by songs, dances, and
a procession, sometimes of persons disguised as the Nine Worthies, whom Shakespeare introduces in a show in *Love's Labor's
Lost*. May Day invariably attracted more formal plays, such
as two anonymous plays on Robin Hood, printed about 1560
and said by the publisher to be "very proper to be played in
May games."

A second dramatic form, related to the folk rituals and plays
because it too was probably derived from primitive celebrations of a life-giving power, was an aristocratic entertainment
that the Middle Ages called a "disguising" and the Renaissance called a "masque." In these entertainments courtiers
amused themselves and sought to express in allegory a high
ideal—in Ben Jonson's words, to "lay hold on more removed
mysteries"—by dressing up, for example, as shepherds or
Moors or Russians, entering a great household, performing
a dance that was sometimes interpreted by a narrator or
Presenter, and then, in a part known as the "revels," dancing
with the ladies. (Apparently for many courtly spectators of this
early sort of "total theater," the dancing, or revels, rather than
the spoken word, was what counted. In 1618 James I inter-

rupted a performance of one of Jonson's masques, by calling out, "Why don't they dance? What did you make me come here for? Devil take you all, dance.") In the masque, as in the Saint George play, there was in the movement from surprise or uncertainty to the celebration of the life-giving force of the powerful person in whose honor the masque was held an implication of fertility, or at least of a united society. The dance at the end of Shakespeare's *Much Ado About Nothing* similarly implies a happy, united society and is a convenient example of the proximity of romantic comedy to the masque. The proximity is even greater at the end of *As You Like It*, where the dance is preceded by the appearance of Hymen, god of marriage. Shakespeare never wrote a court masque, but some of his plays include scenes in which characters engage in a masque. In *Love's Labor's Lost* the king and three courtiers, intending "to parle, to court, and dance," disguise themselves as Russians when they visit the ladies. In *Much Ado About Nothing* Don Pedro and his nobles enter masked and dance with the ladies. *Henry VIII* includes an episode that occurred in 1530 when Henry and some of his courtiers, dressed as shepherds (but splendidly), visited Anne Bullen at Cardinal Wolsey's palace: "*Hautboys. Enter king and others, as masquers, habited like shepherds. . . . They pass directly before the cardinal, and gracefully salute him.*" The chamberlain, acting as the Presenter, explains:

> Because they speak no English, thus they prayed
> To tell your grace: that having heard by fame
> Of this so noble and so fair assembly
> This night to meet here, they could do no less
> (Out of the great respect they bear to beauty)
> But leave their flocks and, under your fair conduct,
> Crave leave to view these ladies and entreat
> An hour of revels with 'em.   (I.iv.65–72)

After the cardinal grants them their wish, the revels begin: "*Choose ladies; King and Anne Bullen,*" and then "*Music. Dance.*" Closely related to these courtly disguisings were spectacular entertainments in great houses, celebrating an event such as a noble wedding. In *The Tempest,* to celebrate an im-

pending marriage, Prospero conjures up a masque of god-
desses, suggestive of fertility. This, and some masquelike scenes
in other late plays, probably was influenced by the masques
that Ben Jonson wrote for the court, beginning in 1605. But
the dissolution of Prospero's show—when he remembers the
plot against him and the masque abruptly vanishes—is different from the dissolution of a court masque. When a court
masque dissolved, the aristocratic performers joined the audience, and the virtues represented in the masque were thus
symbolically bestowed upon the audience; but Prospero's show
abruptly dissolves, occasioning his remarks on the transience
or insubstantiality of all substance (IV.i.148 ff.).

A third kind of dramatic activity that survived from the
Middle Ages into Shakespeare's youth was the miracle play.
(Some scholars distinguish between plays based on saints' lives
and plays based on biblical episodes, calling the former miracle plays and the latter mystery plays. However, no medieval
English play was in its own time called a mystery play.) By
the end of the fourteenth century vast cycles of plays, performed in the streets and sponsored by the craft guilds, had
developed. In a sense, a cycle was one great play, consisting of
as many as forty-eight small plays performed consecutively and
covering the history of the world from the Creation through
the Fall of the Angels, the Creation and Fall of Man, the Incarnation, the Crucifixion, the Resurrection, and Judgment
Day. These cycles were performed early in June on the feast of
Corpus Christi. Because the cycle aimed at celebrating the entire story of Christ, from his incarnation to his redemption of
fallen man, it presented on the stage a remote past that was
also an eternal present. In one play, for example, Christ in-
structs John the Baptist to preach to sinners, and so John turns
to the spectators in front of him, establishing a bond between
the world on the stage and the world of the spectators. This is
not very different from, say, the moment in *As You Like It*
when Duke Senior says—as much to the spectators as to the
characters on the stage—"This wide and universal theater/
Presents more woeful pageants than the scene/Wherein we
play in" (II.vii.136–38).

This tendency to see the stage as intimately related to the daily world of the audience is not the only characteristic that binds the miracle plays to the Elizabethan drama. The saint's play especially used a "comic" pattern of adventures, suffering, and final happiness brought about by the intervention of God, a pattern later secularized (the saint became a prince or princess, God became a god) in romantic drama. Further, although the plot of a cycle was "comic" in that it had a happy ending, it included apparently "tragic" material, such as the murder of Abel and the Slaughter of the Innocents. Such episodes—especially those depicting savage tyranny destroying innocence and thereby ultimately destroying itself or being destroyed by a higher power—probably helped to establish the context of such a scene as Macbeth's slaughter of Macduff's children. Moreover, the comprehensiveness of a miracle cycle's scheme, which required it to mix comedy and tragedy, bequeathed to the Renaissance stage a tradition of mixing the genres. This tradition of mixed dramatic forms (one pre-Shakespearean play, *Cambises,* is called "A Lamentable Tragedy Mixed Full of Pleasant Mirth") distressed those who knew something of classical drama: shortly before Shakespeare began to write for the theater, Sir Philip Sidney lamented that the playwrights of his age wrote "neither right tragedies nor right comedies" but, "mingling kings and clowns," wrote "mongrel tragicomedy." Shakespeare's comedies continued this tradition; they often include threats of death and occasionally (in some of his last plays) death itself. Similarly, his tragedies include comic bits: there are clownish rebels in *2 Henry VI,* a serious history play dealing with violent times, a comic murderer in *Richard III,* a comic gravedigger in *Hamlet,* a fool in *King Lear,* a drunken porter in *Macbeth,* and a comic rural fellow in *Antony and Cleopatra.*

As a child, Shakespeare could easily have seen a cycle of miracle plays. For instance, there were plays done at Coventry, less than twenty miles away, until 1581, when they were suppressed by ecclesiastical authorities who feared popery. But interest in the plays was probably waning by that date, for professional troupes offered better dramatic fare than the amateur companies of guildsmen offered.

A fourth kind of drama that survived into Shakespeare's youth was the morality play, in effect a dramatized sermon, which can be traced to the late fourteenth century. The miracle-play cycles were historical, dramatizing what happened; the morality plays used allegorical figures to dramatize man's chief moral dilemmas as he struggles in a world of deceitful appearances. In *The Castle of Perseverance* (early fifteenth century), for example, a character called Mankind is guided by such figures as Good Angel and Conscience in a struggle against the World, the Flesh, the Devil, the Seven Deadly Sins, and so on. Mankind yields to sin, repents, then relapses; Death enters, but dying Mankind calls for God's mercy, and (as we are told in an epilogue) he is forgiven and allowed to go to heaven. Despite its happy ending, then—and its affinities with, say, *Measure for Measure,* where contrition leads to mercy—the play dramatized suffering and death in this world and thus approaches tragedy. Like *The Castle of Perseverance,* most of the extant morality plays are concerned with the battle for a man's soul (the *psychomachia*), and it is not far-fetched to see their influence in Shakespeare's plays. This is not quite saying that we are getting old wine in new bottles, but it is saying that Shakespeare's tragedies in part draw upon the morality plays for their characters, who, however vividly realized as individuals, are also representatives of types. For instance, despite the good example of the saintly King Duncan, Macbeth yields to Lady Macbeth and the Witches, that is, to forces of evil; Othello faces on one side "the divine Desdemona" and on the other the villainous Iago, who is often associated with diabolic images: late in the play, when Othello realizes that he has been tricked by Iago into murdering Desdemona, he seeks to learn of "that demi-devil/Why he hath thus ensnared my soul and body" (V.ii.300–01). Because the morality play dramatized God's grace, its plot was not tragic; but in its depiction of men making moral decisions and becoming aware of the possible consequences of their mistakes, it borders on tragedy.

Although most morality plays showed inner battles, some were concerned primarily with the coming of death (notably, *Everyman*); others were concerned with political controversy and thus bear some resemblance to Shakespeare's history plays. All the extant moralities except *Everyman* include a good deal of comedy, ranging from physical buffoonery and coarse puns to witty satire, thus continuing the miracle-play tradition of "mongrel tragicomedy." The chief trickster is the Vice, and if Iago is a tragic descendant of that seducer of mankind, the mischievous fools and clowns in Shakespeare's comedies are at least to some degree his comic descendants.

A quotation from one Ralph Willis, who was born the same year as Shakespeare, gives us a good idea of the morality plays and their impact:

In the City of Gloucester the manner is (as I think it is in other like corporations) that when players of interludes come to town, they first attend the Mayor to inform him what nobleman's servants they are, and so to get license for their public playing; and if the Mayor like the actors, or would show respect to their lord and master, he appoints them to play their first play before himself and the Aldermen and Common Council of the City; and that is called the Mayor's Play, where everyone that will comes in without money, the Mayor giving the players a reward as he thinks fit to show respect unto them. At such a play, my father took me with him, and made me stand between his legs, as he sat upon one of the benches where we saw and heard very well. The play was called *The Cradle of Security,* wherein was personated a king or some other great prince with his courtiers of several kinds, amongst which three ladies were in special grace with him; and they keeping him in delights and pleasures, drew him from his graver counsellors, hearing of sermons, and listening to good counsel, and admonitions, that in the end they got him to lie down in a cradle upon the stage, where these three ladies joining in a sweet song rocked him asleep, that he snorted again, and in the meantime closely conveyed under the cloths where withall he was covered, a vizard like a swine's snout upon his face, with three wire chains fastened thereunto, the other end whereof being held severally by those three ladies, who fall to singing again, and then discovered his face, that the spectators might see how they had transformed him, going on with their singing. While all this was acting, there came forth of another door at the farthest end of the stage two old men, the one in blue with a sergeant-at-arms his mace on his shoulder, the other in red with a drawn sword in his hand, and leaning with the other hand upon the other's shoulder, and so these two went along in a soft pace round about by the skirt of the stage till at last they came to the cradle, when all the court was in greatest jollity, and then the foremost old man with his mace struck a fearful blow upon the cradle; whereat all the courtiers with the three ladies and vizard all vanished; and the desolate Prince starting up barefaced, and finding himself thus sent for to judgment, made a lamentable complaint of his miserable case, and so was carried away by wicked spirits. This Prince did personate in the moral the wicked of the world; the three ladies pride, covetousness, and luxury; the two old men, the end of the world and the last judgment. This sight took such impression in me that when I came towards man's estate, it was fresh in my memory as if I had seen it newly acted.

There are three things of special interest here. First, Willis' opening remarks give us an idea of the procedures governing a theatrical company in the provinces. Second, in the punishment of a wicked "desolate Prince" the play anticipates some of the stuff of Elizabethan histories and tragedies. Third, and most important, is Willis' view of the play: today we tend to think of allegorical drama as lifeless, but it made a lasting impression on Willis, who saw it chiefly as a play about people— a king, ladies, counselors, and so on—and only in his final summary as allegory.

As Willis' account indicates, in the sixteenth century the morality play was performed by professionals. The morality play was closely related to a type called the "interlude," a short play, often with the structure, characters, and comedy of a morality play, that was performed in a great house, especially during a holiday season. Possibly the chief difference is that an interlude was usually shorter and required fewer characters than a morality play. (The name *interlude* seems to suggest that the play was performed between two parts of a banquet.) The morality play abounded in vigorous men of this world, and it is not surprising that in the sixteenth century there were many short plays in which exuberant worldly characters were the center of interest: these plays, performed as entertainments in a banquet-hall, sometimes became essentially a dramatized joke rather than a dramatized sermon, and then of course the distinction between interlude and morality play becomes clear.

A fifth kind of theatrical activity that exerted an influence on Shakespeare was the drama of the schools and universities. In the sixteenth century students read Roman drama and occasionally performed it. Schoolmasters, with Roman plays in mind, wrote plays to help their students improve their enunciation, poise, and skill in disputation. Neo-Latin as well as English plays were written, and though no academic drama has much literary or theatrical excellence, the fact that in Shakespeare's day some university graduates wrote for the popular stage indicates that the academic drama exerted at least some influence on the popular drama. (The specific influences of Plautus and Terence on comedy, and of Seneca on tragedy, are discussed on pp. 78–82, 145–47.)

Brief mention should be made here of the professional drama of Shakespeare's immediate predecessors and contemporaries, notably John Lyly, Thomas Kyd, and Christopher Marlowe. Lyly's rather precious comedies, performed by a children's company chiefly in the 1580's, with their formal groupings and elegant witty debates and with their contrasts between scenes of delightfully absurd romantic lovers and scenes of low comedy, must have helped Shakespeare—and yet Shakespeare's comedy is still distinctively his own, more humane, less allegorical, less satirical, less situational or static, and more narrative than Lyly's, and more thoughtful and better articulated than anything on the earlier popular stage. Similarly, though about 1589 Kyd apparently gave English popular tragedy a strong sense of a coherent plot (for example, ironically juxtaposed scenes instead of more loosely connected episodes), and Marlowe from about 1589 until his death in 1593 gave English tragedy heroes who speak a splendid blank verse worthy of heroes, these two writers themselves were deeply indebted to earlier dramatic traditions: Kyd to

Senecan drama and Marlowe to the morality play. Shakespeare's achievement soon became distinctive, indebted to but
far outstripping his early contemporaries. The drama of
Shakespeare's age is discussed in the sections on Shakespeare's
comedies, histories, and tragedies, but for the moment it may
be amusing to hear Stephen Gosson's puritanical attack on
these genres as they existed six or eight years before Shakespeare set to work, when romances, continental short fiction
(*novelle*), and chronicles provided much of the stuff of popular drama. The passages are all from Gosson's *Plays Con-
futed in Five Actions* (1582). First, Gosson on comedy, which
he sees as immoral. Judging from the plays that survive, it
may be said that Gosson grossly overstates the immorality, but
he gives us a fair sense of the chief theme of much comedy:

> The groundwork of comedies is love, cozenage, flattery, bawdry, sly
> conveyance of whoredom; the persons, cooks, queans, knaves, bawds,
> parasites, courtezans, lecherous old men, amorous young men. . . .
> Comedies so tickle our senses . . . that they make us lovers of
> laughter and pleasure without any mean. . . . What schooling is
> this?

Next, Gosson on tragedy, which he sees not as valuable but as
debilitating. Again he gives us a sense of the chief action:

> The beholding of troubles and miserable slaughters that are in
> tragedies drive us to immoderate sorrow, heaviness, womanish weep-
> ing and mourning, whereby we become lovers of dumps, and lamenta-
> tion, both enemies to fortitude.

Finally, Gosson on history plays, which he sees as distortions
of history and therefore vicious. His observations are surely
right, though his implications are surely wrong:

> If a true history be taken in hand, it is made like our shadows,
> longest at the rising and falling of the sun, shortest of all at high
> noon. For the poets drive it most commonly unto such points as
> may best show the majesty of their pen in tragical speeches, or set
> the hearers agog with discourses of love, or paint a few antics to
> fit their own humors with scoffs and taunts, or wring in a show to
> furnish the stage when it is too bare. When the matter of itself

comes short of this, they follow the practice of the cobbler, and set their teeth to the leather to pull it out. So was the history of Caesar and Pompey, and the play of the Fabii at the Theater, both amplified there, where the drums might walk or the pen ruffle. When the history swelled and ran too high for the number of the persons that should play it, the poet with Proteus [that is, Procrustes] cut the same fit to his own measure; when it afforded no pomp at all, he brought it to the rack to make it serve.

Had Gosson written again some thirty years later, when Shakespeare had completed his career, he probably would have seen no reason to alter his words. To a hostile eye, Shakespeare would only seem to be doing better what his predecessors had done (and therefore he was the more dangerous). Subsequent pages will try to call attention to his distinction.

5

Style and Structure

Perhaps "style" would be sufficient as a heading here because, if broadly and deeply conceived, it takes in everything: the choice of words and their arrangement in lines, metrics, prose rhythms, and even the choice of plots and of characters. Though style is often contrasted with content, as though it were a decorative treatment of meaning, it can be argued that style (for example, Latinate versus Anglo-Saxon diction, or the inclusion versus the exclusion of comic material in a tragic plot) is inherently part of the meaning. Cardinal Newman put it thus: "Thought and meaning are inseparable from each other. Matter and expression are parts of one: style is a thinking out into language."

NONVERBAL DEVICES

Because Shakespeare was a dramatist, his style is a thinking out not only into language (which includes diction, grammar, images, meter, and rhythm) but also into costumes, sound effects, gestures, and even silences. The use of costumes as a part of the dramatist's language has already been discussed (pp. 27–29). To the examples of Hamlet's "inky cloak," which separates him from the opulently dressed courtiers, and the fresh clothing in which Lear is garbed after his madness, can be added the broader matter of disguises—for example, the monk's robe worn by Duke Vincentio in *Measure for Measure* and Rosalind's and Viola's male attire in *As You Like It* and

41

Twelfth Night; these are removed at the ends of the plays, when the truth is at last revealed and the characters can again be fully themselves. In short, the removal of disguises *says* something.

Sound effects too communicate meaning. Perhaps the most obvious example is the sound of the storm in *King Lear*, which is a reflection of Lear's disordered kingdom, disordered family, and disordered mind. A little less obvious is the noise of cannon in *Hamlet*. Early in the play cannon are fired when Claudius drinks deeply, and the reverberation of the noise to the heavens suggests Claudius' power, vulgarity, and arrogance; later in the play Claudius again orders the cannon to sound, this time when he hypocritically drinks to Hamlet before the fencing match; at the end of the play the cannon are once again ordered to be fired, not by Claudius but by Fortinbras, and now in tribute to Hamlet, who has earned "the soldiers' music."

Gestures are also an important part of the dramatist's language. For example, King Lear kneels before his daughter Cordelia for a benediction (IV.vii.57–59), an act of humility that contrasts with his earlier speeches banishing her and that contrasts also with a comparable gesture, his ironic kneeling before Regan (II.iv.152). Northumberland's failure to kneel before King Richard II (III.iii.71–72) speaks volumes, as Richard notices. In the first act of *Coriolanus* Volumnia hopes that her son will defeat Aufidius "and tread upon his neck," but in the last act it is Aufidius who, according to the stage direction, *"stands on"* Coriolanus. *Coriolanus* also affords an example of the importance of dramatic silence; before the protagonist yields to his mother's entreaties (V.iii.182), there is this stage direction: *"Holds her by the hand, silent."* Another example of "speech in dumbness" occurs in *Macbeth*, when Macduff learns that his wife and children have been murdered. He is silent at first, as Malcolm's speech indicates: "What, man! Ne'er pull your hat upon your brows./Give sorrow words" (IV.iii.208 ff.). In the abdication scene of *Richard II* (IV.i), Richard speaks 132 lines against Bolingbroke's 14, and Bolingbroke's forbidding silence—which Richard comments on when he addresses the "silent king"—is part of Boling-broke's character and part of the meaning of the play. A play-wright's language, clearly, is not simply verbal language. Even an actor's position on the stage may have meaning. In *Romeo and Juliet* (III.v) the lovers share a scene *"aloft,"* suggesting their exaltation. Romeo then *"goeth down,"* and Juliet, look-ing down on him, prophetically says, "Methinks I see thee, now thou art so low,/As one dead in the bottom of a tomb" (III.v.55–56). Something of the reverse movement is indicated by a stage direction in *Antony and Cleopatra* when Antony leaves "this dull world" and dies: *"They heave Antony aloft to Cleopatra"* (IV.xv.37).

PROSE

Of course, when we think of Shakespeare's style we think primarily of his language, both the poetry and the prose. Al-though two of the plays (*Richard II* and *King John*) have no prose at all, about half the others have at least one fourth of the dialogue in prose, and some have notably more: *Troilus and Cressida,* one third; *1 Henry IV* and *2 Henry IV,* about half; *As You Like It* and *Twelfth Night,* a little more than half; *Much Ado About Nothing,* about three fourths; and *The Merry Wives of Windsor,* about nine tenths. All these plays were probably written between 1597 and 1602, in what might be called (with exaggeration, of course) Shakespeare's "prose period." During this time Shakespeare was perhaps de-veloping as a poet, learning how to make significant rather than unvarying use of poetry, and learning how to bring his language closer to an approximation of speech. (But we should remember that despite Molière's joke about M. Jourdain, who was amazed to learn that he spoke prose, prose is not what most of us speak. We normally utter repetitive, shapeless, and often ungrammatical torrents; prose is something very differ-ent—a sort of literary imitation of speech at its most coherent.)

Today we perhaps think of prose as "natural" for comedies, but Greek, Roman, and early English comedies were written in verse. In fact, prose was not generally considered a literary medium in England until the late fifteenth century; Chaucer tells even his bawdy stories in verse. By the end of the 1580's, however, prose had established itself on the English comic stage with the plays of John Lyly, comedies that used an extremely patterned and figurative prose and that were designed for a courtly rather than a popular audience. In tragedy, Marlowe had made some use of prose, not simply in the speeches of clownish servants but even in the speech of a tragic hero, Doctor Faustus. With the notable exceptions of Lyly and Marlowe, however, dramatic prose before Shakespeare is scarcely memorable. It was normally used only for special circumstances: (1) letters and proclamations, to set them off from the poetic dialogue; (2) mad characters, to indicate that normal thinking has become disordered; and (3) low comedy, or speeches uttered by clowns even when they are not being comic. Shakespeare made use of these conventions (to the second group—mad characters such as Lear, Ophelia, and Lady Macbeth—can be added Lepidus when he is drunk in *Antony and Cleopatra*), but he also went far beyond them. He sometimes used prose for (4) cynical commentary, such as Thersites' remarks in *Troilus and Cressida* or Casca's report in *Julius Caesar* of Caesar's reluctant refusal of the crown (I.ii); (5) scenes of ordinary life, such as those of Prince Hal at his ease in the tavern in *1 Henry IV;* (6) scenes of courtship, such as those between Beatrice and Benedick in *Much Ado About Nothing,* and Rosalind and Orlando (though Orlando does not realize that courtship is going on) in *As You Like It,* and even between King Henry and Katherine of France in *Henry V.* Moreover, sometimes a scene begins in prose and then shifts into verse as the emotion is heightened; or conversely, a scene shifts from verse to prose when a speaker is lowering the emotional level (as when Brutus speaks in the forum). Thus it is not enough to say that low characters speak prose, high characters speak verse; in *Richard II,* for example, the gardeners (III.iv) and the groom (V.v) speak verse, and in other plays monarchs often speak prose.

Nor is Shakespeare's prose prosaic, used only to represent ordinary conversation or to communicate necessary information. Hamlet's prose includes not only small talk with Rosencrantz and Guildenstern but princely reflections on "What a piece of work is a man" (II.ii). In conversation with Ophelia Hamlet shifts from light talk in verse to a passionate prose denunciation of women (III.ii), though the shift to prose here is perhaps intended to suggest the possibility of madness—at least Ophelia immediately concludes that Hamlet's "noble mind is here o'erthrown."

Below are examples of Shakespeare's prose, showing something of its structure and its range. The first is from Brutus' funeral oration in *Julius Caesar*:

Romans, countrymen, and lovers, hear me for my cause, and be silent, that you may hear. Believe me for mine honor, and have respect to mine honor, that you may believe. Censure me in your wisdom, and awake your senses, that you may the better judge.

(III.ii.13–17)

Despite its apparent simplicity, this prose speech is elaborately constructed. Notice Brutus' use of isocolon (successive phrases or clauses of approximately equal length) in three successive sentences, each approximately equal in length and each with three clauses:

hear me for my cause,/and be silent,/that you may hear.
Believe me for mine honor,/and have respect to mine honor,/that you may believe.
Censure me in your wisdom,/and awake your senses,/that you may the better judge.

Notice, too, the rather complacent repetitions: "hear . . . hear," "mine honor . . . mine honor," "Censure . . . senses." Later in the speech there are alliterative lines: "*b*ase . . . *b*e . . . *b*ondman," "*r*ude . . . *R*oman." The speech is fully in accord with Brutus' conception of himself as a man who balances things thoughtfully in his mind. But there is something repelling in the sixfold repetition (in forty-two words) of "me," "my," "me," "mine," "mine," "me."

Brutus' prose can be contrasted with a passage from *Hamlet*, V.ii. When Horatio offers to make excuses if Hamlet wishes to avoid the duel with Laertes, Hamlet replies:

Not a whit, we defy augury. There is special providence in the fall of a sparrow. If it be now, 'tis not to come; if it be not to come, it will be now; if it be not now, yet it will come. The readiness is all. Since no man of aught he leaves knows, what is't to leave betimes? Let be.   (V.ii.221–26)

Of the sixty-two words in the speech, only seven are of more than one syllable. On the whole the diction is colloquial (note especially "Not a whit"), but there is the solemn echo of the Bible ("special providence in the fall of a sparrow"), and the clauses are balanced. The speech is simple and meditative, yet strong-willed in the final "Let be."

There is no need here to quote examples of what are in effect comic prose monologues, such as Touchstone's speech on lying (*As You Like It*, V.iv.69–82) or Falstaff's discourse on honor (*1 Henry IV*, V.i.127–41). What is especially worth noting is that although Shakespeare's characters occasionally utter the garbled chaos that is our daily talk—such as the Nurse in *Romeo and Juliet*, "Well, sir, my mistress is the sweetest lady. Lord, Lord! When 'twas a little prating thing—O, there is a nobleman in town" (II.iv.203–05)—for the most part even his lowest characters speak coherently, and each seems to speak his appropriate idiom. Here is the simple country fellow who tells Cleopatra that he has brought the asp with which she will commit suicide:

Truly I have him; but I would not be the party that should desire you to touch him, for his biting is immortal: those that do die of it do seldom or never recover.   (V.ii.245–48)

The clown has an odd idea of death, and he says "immortal" for "mortal"; yet Cleopatra *does* become immortal, and though the entire speech has an impressive coherence, it somehow conveys the clown's simplicity.

POETRY

Verse drama in England goes back to the Middle Ages, but truly poetic drama is probably no older than George Peele's *The Arraignment of Paris* (about 1580). For the most part the drama of the seventies presented such harrowing stuff as this passage from *Cambises* (about 1569), written in fourteeners, or pairs of rhyming lines of fourteen syllables each:

> I feel myself a-dying now, of life bereft am I,
> And death hath caught me with his dart, for want of blood I die.
> Thus gasping here on ground I lie; for nothing do I care;
> A just reward for my misdeeds my death doth plain declare.

This passage is not meant to be comic, though it sounds rather like Bottom's words when he impersonates the dying Pyramus in *A Midsummer Night's Dream* (V.i).

By Shakespeare's day, however, rhyme no longer dominated poetic drama; a finer medium, blank verse, had been adopted. But before looking at Elizabethan unrhymed verse, a few things should be said about the chief uses of rhyme in Shakespeare's plays. (1) Emotional heightening at the end of a blank-verse speech is often indicated by a couplet (a pair of rhyming lines). (2) Characters sometimes speak a couplet as they leave the stage. (3) Except in the latest plays, scenes or acts fairly often conclude with a couplet, and sometimes, as in *Richard II*, I.i.18–19, the entrance of a new character within a scene is preceded by a couplet, which wraps up the earlier portion of that scene. (4) Speeches of two characters occasionally are linked by rhyme, most notably in *Romeo and Juliet*, I.v. 95–108, where the lovers speak a sonnet between them; elsewhere a taunting reply occasionally rhymes with the previous speaker's last line. (5) Speeches with sententious or gnomic remarks are sometimes in rhyme, as in the duke's speech in *Othello* (I.iii.199–206) and the king's speech in *All's Well That Ends Well* (II.iii.126–45). (6) Speeches with sardonic mockery are sometimes in rhyme—for example, Iago's speech on women in *Othello* (II.i.146–58)—and sometimes conclude with an em-

phatic couplet, as in Bolingbroke's speech on comforting words
in *Richard II* (I.iii.301–02). (7) Some characters are associated
with rhyme—for example, the fairies in *A Midsummer Night's
Dream* and to a lesser degree Faulconbridge in *King John*
and Apemantus in *Timon of Athens,* though because Faulconbridge and Apemantus are given to mockery their rhymes perhaps properly belong in the previous category. (8) In the early
plays, especially *The Comedy of Errors* and *The Taming of
the Shrew,* comic scenes that in later plays would be in prose
are in jingling rhymes. (9) Prologues, choruses, plays-within-
the-play, inscriptions, vows, epilogues, and so on, are often in
rhyme, and of course the songs in plays are rhymed. The play-
within-the-play in *Hamlet,* for example, is written in an older
style to set it off from the language of the play itself:

> Full thirty times hath Phoebus' cart gone round
> Neptune's salt wash and Tellus' orbèd ground,
> And thirty dozen moons with borrowed sheen
> About the world have times twelve thirties been,
> Since love our hearts, and Hymen did our hands,
> Unite commutual in most sacred bands.   (III.ii.158–63)

The plays with the highest percentage of rhymed dialogue are
(in decreasing order) *Love's Labor's Lost, A Midsummer
Night's Dream, The Comedy of Errors, Richard II,* and
Romeo and Juliet. Of these five, all but *The Comedy of Errors*
were written about 1594–96, which is probably also the period
during which Shakespeare wrote many of his sonnets. Most of
the rhyme in Shakespeare's last plays (with the exception of
Pericles) is not in dialogue properly speaking but in songs,
choruses, or a masque (*The Tempest*). Broadly speaking, then,
after the "prose period" of about 1597–1602 Shakespeare
tended to use less and less rhyme in dialogue.

But it is neither prose nor rhyme that comes to mind when
we first think of Shakespeare's medium: it is blank verse, unrhymed iambic pentameter (in a mechanically exact line there
are five feet, each foot with two syllables, every second syllable
accented). The first speech in *A Midsummer Night's Dream* is
an example of blank verse:

Now, fair Hippolyta, our nuptial hour
Draws on apace. Four happy days bring in
Another moon; but, O, methinks, how slow
This old moon wanes! She lingers my desires,
Like to a stepdame, or a dowager,
Long withering out a young man's revenue.   (I.i.1–6)

As this passage shows, Shakespeare's blank verse is not mechanically unvarying. Though the predominant foot is the iamb (customarily indicated by ‿′), there are numerous variations. In the first line the stress can be placed on "fair," as the regular metrical pattern suggests, but it is likely that "Now" gets almost as much emphasis; probably in the second line "Draws" is more heavily emphasized than "on," giving us a trochee (indicated by ′‿); and in the fourth line each word in the phrase "This old moon wanes" is probably stressed fairly heavily, conveying by two spondees (each indicated by ′′) the oppressive tedium that Theseus feels.

Blank verse, first printed in England in 1557 in Surrey's posthumously published translation of parts of Virgil's *Aeneid,* was first used in a play in 1561, in Thomas Sackville and Thomas Norton's *Gorboduc.* But if *Gorboduc* thus looks forward to Marlowe and Shakespeare, it also looks backward in its heavy alliteration, its tendency to use paired lines (much of it seems to be couplets without rhymes), and its formal balance, as the first speech of the play indicates:

The silent night, that brings the quiet pause
From painful travails of the weary day,
Prolongs my careful thoughts, and makes me blame
The slow Aurore, that so for love or shame
Doth long delay to show her blushing face.
And now the day renews my griefull plaint.

The first line introduces a favorite Renaissance device, a disyllabic adjective followed by a monosyllabic noun ("silent night," "quiet pause"); this device reappears in the next line ("weary day") and yet again in all but one of the following lines ("careful thoughts," "blushing face," "griefull plaint"). Elsewhere lines are often end-stopped (that is, there is a distinct syntactical pause at the end of the line), as the second speech in *Gorboduc* reveals:

> My gracious lady and my mother dear,
> Pardon my grief for your so grievèd mind,
> To ask what cause tormenteth so your heart.

Alliteration is abundant: in the first speech "*p*ause," "*p*ainful," "*P*rolongs," "*s*low," "*s*o," "*D*oth," "*d*elay," "*d*ay," "*p*laint"; in the second speech "*g*racious," "*g*rief," "*g*rievèd." In the late 1580's Marlowe changed all this, partly by somewhat reducing the amount of alliteration and partly by joining phrases and clauses with *and* so that a sentence ran to a dozen or so lines. Most important, Marlowe was a poet, not a versifier, and he gave to blank verse a richness that inevitably drew later poets to the form.

In Shakespeare's early plays much of the poetry is end-stopped, but he later developed the ability to write iambic-pentameter verse paragraphs (rather than lines) that give the illusion of speech. His chief techniques are (1) running the thought beyond the single line; (2) occasionally substituting another foot for an iambic foot; (3) varying the position of the chief pause within a line; (4) adding an occasional unstressed syllable at the end of a line, a so-called feminine ending; (5) and beginning or ending a speech with a half-line. In addition, Shakespeare's speeches often suggest the nature of the speaker, whereas in *Gorboduc* all the speeches sound alike, as though they issued from a single undefined mouth. In *Hamlet* the king ceremoniously—that is, rather formally—addresses his court in a long sentence whose meaning is suspended until near the end:

> Though yet of Hamlet our dear brother's death
> The memory be green, and that it us befitted
> To bear our hearts in grief, and our whole kingdom
> To be contracted in one brow of woe,
> Yet so far hath discretion fought with nature
> That we with wisest sorrow think on him
> Together with remembrance of ourselves.   (I.ii.1–7)

Later in the scene Claudius speaks more intimately:

And now, Laertes, what's the news with you?
You told us of some suit. What is't, Laertes?
You cannot speak of reason to the Dane
And lose your voice. What wouldst thou beg, Laertes,
That shall not be my offer, not thy asking?   (I.ii.42–46)

Notice the short sentences and the ingratiating repetition of
the name "Laertes," to whom the speech is addressed. Notice,
too, the shift from the royal "us" in the second line to the
more intimate "my" in the last line, and from "you" in the
first three lines to the more intimate "thou" and "thy" in the
last two lines.

Macbeth, distressed by the doctor's inability to cure Lady
Macbeth and by the imminent battle, addresses some of his remarks to the doctor and others to the servant who is arming
him. The entire speech, with its pauses, interruptions, and ir-
resolution (in "Pull't off, I say," Macbeth orders the servant
to remove the armor he has been putting on him), catches
Macbeth's disintegration:

Throw physic to the dogs, I'll none of it.
Come, put mine armor on. Give me my staff.
Seyton, send out.—Doctor, the thanes fly from me.—
Come, sir, dispatch. If thou couldst, doctor, cast
The water of my land, find her disease
And purge it to a sound and pristine health,
I would applaud thee to the very echo,
That should applaud again.—Pull't off, I say.—
What rhubarb, senna, or what purgative drug,
Would scour these English hence? Hear'st thou of them?
                                                    (V.iii.47–56)

Duke Frederick in *As You Like It* is disappointed to find
that a young man who has performed nobly is the son of an
enemy:

I would thou hadst been son to some man else.
The world esteemed thy father honorable,
But I did find him still mine enemy.
Thou shouldst have better pleased me with this deed
Hadst thou descended from another house.

But fare thee well; thou art a gallant youth;
I would thou hadst told me of another father.   (I.ii.220–26)

Duke Frederick's lines are end-stopped, but the effect is not
one of monotony. Rather, the regular pauses and the repetition of part of the first line in the last ("I would thou hadst")
and the continual turning back ("But," "But") convey the ten-
sion of conflicting emotions and the speaker's unwillingness
to let his spirit generously expand.

Finally the Nurse in *Romeo and Juliet* babbles in blank
verse that Juliet will soon be fourteen years old:

Come Lammas Eve at night shall she be fourteen.
Susan and she (God rest all Christian souls!)
Were of an age. Well, Susan is with God;
She was too good for me. But, as I said,
On Lammas Eve at night shall she be fourteen;
That shall she, marry; I remember it well.
'Tis since the earthquake now eleven years;
And she was weaned (I never shall forget it),
Of all the days of the year, upon that day;
For I had then laid wormwood to my dug,
Sitting in the sun under the dovehouse wall.
My lord and you were then at Mantua.
Nay, I do bear a brain.   (I.iii.17–29)

Blank verse, then, can be much more than unrhymed iambic
pentameter, and even within a single play Shakespeare's blank
verse often consists of several styles, depending on the speaker
and on the speaker's emotion at the moment. Of course, much
depends on the length of the speech: a speech of a single line
has a different tone from a long speech, even though the metrical pattern in both is iambic. It should be mentioned, too, that
although the difference between verse and prose is clearly evident on a printed page, spectators in the theater are rarely
aware of the shift; almost always they hear not verse or prose
but people talking in a way that seems right for the situation.
And although in real life people do not talk in verse, their
speech—especially when they are passionate—tends to be
rhythmical. So we can say that in Shakespeare we get "natural" utterances in the sense that the utterances—verse as well

as prose—are the perfect expression of what our speech would be if we were fully the masters of it.

FIGURATIVE LANGUAGE

Another departure from ordinary usage common in Shakespeare (and in almost all poets) is the use of tropes, or figurative language. When, in I.i, Iago urges Roderigo to "poison [Othello's] delight" he is not advocating the literal use of poison, and when he urges Roderigo to "plague him with flies" he is suggesting not that Roderigo open a bag of flies in Othello's presence but that he somehow distress Othello with trivial, irritating things. The words, though they strike us as natural, are clearly not used in their literal or normal sense.

Shakespeare's early figurative language, however, is sometimes ostentatious. The figures often seem to be tacked on, elaborate embellishments of an idea rather than the inevitable presentation of the idea itself. For example, Queen Tamora's lover in *Titus Andronicus,* an early play, describes the queen's good fortune thus:

Now climbeth Tamora Olympus' top,
Safe out of fortune's shot, and sits aloft,
Secure of thunder's crack or lightning flash,
Advanced above pale envy's threat'ning reach.
As when the golden sun salutes the morn,
And having gilt the ocean with his beams,
Gallops the zodiac in his glistering coach,
And overlooks the highest-peering hills;
So Tamora.   (II.i.1–9)

The last five lines seem tacked on to the first four, an embellishment rather than an integral part of the speech.

Shakespeare's later figurative language appears more natural, less decorative, and more integral. There are exceptions, of course, but on the whole his progress was something like Berowne's in *Love's Labor's Lost.* Near the end of the play (V.ii) Berowne says that he will forswear "taffeta phrases" and "Three-piled hyperboles, spruce affectation,/Figures pedantical" and will substitute for them "russet yeas and honest kersey noes" (homespun woolen cloth). The expression "russet yeas and honest kersey noes" of course is itself as figurative as "taffeta phrases," and Shakespeare never abandoned figures, though he curbed his exuberance.

Figures commonly add sensory content—compare "plague him with flies" with "bother him with trivialities"—but of course not all sensory words are figurative. When, in I.ii, Othello commands the Venetians to "Keep up your bright swords," the phrase "bright swords" refers literally (rather than figuratively) to the swords they are flourishing. All such sensory words, whether figurative or literal, can be called images, though there is a tendency in criticism to concentrate on figurative rather than literal images, neglecting, for example, the abundant literal talk about blood in *Julius Caesar* while dwelling on metaphors. One can deplore the neglect of the literal, especially in the study of drama, which involves people carrying swords, holding up bloody hands, and so on, but one can understand why critics have tended to dwell on those images involving metaphors, similes, and the host of other figurative uses of language that are enumerated in handbooks of rhetoric.

There are at least three important uses of imagery. First, it can afford delight in itself, giving a sense of the nature of things. By saying "Keep up your bright swords" rather than "Calm yourselves" or "Do not fight," Othello gives us a rich sense of the concrete world—both its singularity and its multiplicity. As Coleridge said, Shakespeare "by metaphors and figures involves in the thing considered a universe of past and possible experiences." At the end of the first scene in *Hamlet* Horatio talks of the coming of the dawn:

> But look, the morn in russet mantle clad
> Walks o'er the dew of yon high eastward hill.   (I.i.166–67)

Horatio's lines tell us of the time of day, but the images serve a further dramatic purpose. The scene begins at midnight, and is full of uncertainties, including two harrowing encounters with a ghost; then it becomes early morning, and the suggestion of light implies the coming of order and harmony. But the image of "in russet mantle clad" precisely qualifies this light: dawn is personified not as the bright and sunny Aurora but as a peasant in his workaday mantle of coarse grayish-brown material. The morning and the daily business of living dispel the darkness, but full light has not yet come to the shadowy tragic world. There is, then, something sharp and precisely right (and therefore delightful) about the description of this particular kind of morning. We may never have noticed such a morning, and the image serves to enrich our sense of the world.

Second, imagery can help to characterize the speaker. Not every line and image in Shakespeare does this, of course. The passage just quoted from *Hamlet* is not especially typical of Horatio's manner. If we were to look for lines that characterize Horatio, we would probably choose less "poetic" or lyrical and more ironic lines, such as his dry "a truant disposition," when Hamlet asks him why he is not at the university, or, since Horatio is a "scholar," his rather bookish speech in I.i. in which he refers to Caesar as "the mightiest Julius," to the moon as "the moist star," and to the ocean as "Neptune's empire." Horatio's speech about the dawn exists not to reveal anything about Horatio but to tell us about the time of the day and the particular quality of the morning, and to balance the appearance of the Ghost with a sense of nature's divinity. But innumerable images in Shakespeare do help to define character. The tragic heroes, for example, often speak in hyperbole, a figure appropriate to their greatness. Othello says that were it not for the love of Desdemona he would not confine himself "for the sea's worth"; nine months gone by are "nine moons wasted"; caves are "anters vast"; waves are "hills of seas Olympus-high." Iago says that Othello brags and tells "fantastical lies," but this is a villain's cynical view, unsupported by anything else in the play. Against Othello's hyperbolic and exotic language are Iago's figures that diminish men. Iago's allusion to flies has already been noted; other animals are commonly in his mind: a faithful servant is an "ass," Othello is "an old black ram," Desdemona is a "white ewe," their offspring will "neigh," and the lovers "are making the beast with two backs." All these words occur in the first 115 lines of the first scene. In later scenes Iago alludes to women as wildcats, to Cassio and Desdemona as "goats, . . . monkeys, . . . wolves," and to a married man as "yoked" (that is, an ox). In contrast to Othello, Iago is the sort of man who sees people chiefly as sexual or stupid beasts. Interestingly, however, once Iago has succeeded in infecting Othello's mind, Othello too begins to use such images, speaking of "goats and monkeys," "toads," "aspics' tongues," "crocodile," and "flies."

Finally, images often help to define the theme of the play. (A few words about this third use of imagery are included in the discussion of images of rising and falling in *Richard II* on p. 129 and in the discussion of images of light, dark, and speed in *Romeo and Juliet* on p. 151.) In *Othello,* diabolic images ("hell," "devil," "perdition") are at first associated with Iago and then, as Othello comes under Iago's power, with Othello. As S. L. Bethell points out in *Shakespeare Survey 5,* there are sixty-four such images in Othello. Of course, not all the occurrences are of equal significance—for example, the first diabolic image, Iago's assertion that Cassio is "almost damned in a fair wife," is trivial when compared with Iago's

> I have't! It is engendered! Hell and night
> Must bring this monstrous birth to the world's light.
>
> (I.iii.392–93)

But though the statistics must be interpreted with caution, they do add up to something. Here are Bethell's calculations. First, the diabolic images steadily increase from the first act to the last: the figures for the five acts are 10, 11, 13, 14, 16, respectively. Furthermore, the disposition of these images according to speaker is interesting. As Bethell explains,

Iago has only his fair proportion of diabolic imagery, yet we undoubtedly gain the impression that in this play the theme of hell, as it were, originates with him and is passed to Othello later as Iago succeeds in dominating his mind. Statistics show this impression to be well-founded. In Act I Iago has eight diabolic images and

Othello none; in Act II he has six and Othello one. The change comes in Act III, where Iago drops to three and Othello rises to nine. In Act IV Iago has only one while Othello has ten, and in Act V Iago has none and Othello six. It all begins, then, with Iago.*

These images, of course, help to define the speakers: Iago is a nasty figure given (like the devil) to destructiveness; Othello is a man who at least for a while becomes his instrument. But the images also go beyond character and help to define the theme: on one level *Othello* is a domestic tragedy, a play about a man who kills his wife; on another level it is about the mysterious power of evil, of the sort associated with the devil—an evil that hates what is good (Coleridge aptly speaks of Iago's "motiveless malignity") and sometimes brings it to material and spiritual destruction.

Another example of imagery that goes beyond characterization and helps to establish theme is the storm imagery in *King Lear*. A storm literally takes place in the middle of the play, but the storm also has symbolic implications. As early as I.ii Gloucester speaks of disturbances in nature and of "all ruinous disorder"; Lear calls down "Blasts and fogs" (I.iv.301) and the "nimble lightnings" (II.iv.162) upon Goneril. As the break with his only remaining daughter, Regan, is widened and Lear is almost driven to madness, the stage direction *"Storm and tempest"* appears (II.iv.280), followed in three lines by Lear's explicit fear that he "shall go mad." Thus, as has already been mentioned, the chaos in Lear's family, the chaos in nature, and the chaos in Lear's mind are all linked. A few lines later Cornwall says that it is "a wild night," and still later we see the deranged Lear in a stormy, deranged world. Lear himself equates the macrocosm and the microcosm, the great world and the little world of man, when he speaks of "the tempest in my mind." Only a few of the storm images have been commented on here; but the more one studies the play the more one sees that the images are not decorative but

---

* S. L. Bethell, "Shakespeare's Imagery: The Diabolic Images in *Othello*," *Shakespeare Survey 5*, ed. Allardyce Nicoll (New York: Cambridge University Press, 1952), p. 69.

integral; if they were removed from the play, and if the storm itself were removed, *King Lear* would say something entirely different.

Of course, no spectator can be fully aware of all the implications of all Shakespeare's images; nor can a reader be, unless he takes notes line by line. Shakespeare himself probably was not conscious of the patterns of images he created, and he would have been surprised by Bethell's statistics on *Othello* or by a list of the storm images in *King Lear*. But if these statistics would have surprised him, it is probably only because he did not put the images in one by one; rather, he imagined his characters and his plots and his themes so fully that the images inevitably came in the speeches. Though we may be unaware of them, the images, both figurative and literal (as for instance the blood in *Julius Caesar*), have a profound effect; they work along with the nonverbal imagery of visible stage properties, gestures, and costumes (see pp. 27–29 and 42–43 for a discussion of such imagery).

CHARACTER AND PLOT

When we think of a play, however—unless we have been corrupted by education—we first think not of images or themes but of characters and plot. Shakespeare's powers of characterization are so great that we may sometimes feel, like Alexander Pope, that "had all the speeches been printed without the names of the persons, I believe one might have applied them with certainty to every speaker." Of course this is not always true, partly because Shakespeare was sometimes concerned not with characterization but with establishing (for example) time or locale and partly because a good many First and Second Gentlemen have no character. Moreover, sometimes part of the point is that the characters are *not* distinct. The lovers in *A Midsummer Night's Dream,* all of whom quite naturally think that their experiences are unique, often sound very much alike, and this similarity—this uniformity of which the lovers are comically unaware—is surely part of

Shakespeare's meaning. On the whole, however, Shakespeare's characters do have a roundness, an identity.

What a character is depends on at least two things: what he says and does, and what other characters say about him and what they do. We have already seen how prose and verse reveal character. Relationships between characters also perform this function, as can be seen by an illustration from *Hamlet*. Like Hamlet, Laertes has lost his father. Hamlet has a chance to avenge his father's death when Claudius is praying (III.iii), but he passes it by; Laertes says that if his father's killer were within reach, he would "cut his throat i' th' church" (IV.vii. 127); Hamlet feels "the dread of something after death" (III.i. 78); Laertes says "Conscience and grace to the profoundest pit!/I dare damnation" (IV.v.133–34); and so on. Laertes is prone to action—but he is less scrupulous than Hamlet and he easily becomes a cat's-paw for Claudius. As he is dying Laertes confesses, "I am justly killed with mine own treachery" (V.ii. 308). If Hamlet is slow to act, it is at least partly because he is more imaginative than Laertes. What Hamlet *is*, then, is partly clarified by his contrast to Laertes, who is another young man also concerned about avenging his father's death. Fortinbras, yet another young man with whom Hamlet is contrasted, is also fatherless; indeed, his father died at the hands of Hamlet's father. Fortinbras, of course, is not an avenger, but he can fight for a worthless patch of ground, while Hamlet, with an urgent cause, delays. But Fortinbras' very willingness to sacrifice thousands of lives "even for an eggshell" undermines the importance of action. A third character, the stoical Horatio, also helps to define Hamlet. Hamlet admires Horatio's dispassionateness (III.ii); yet this very dispassionateness makes Horatio a lesser figure, a man who presumably even in Hamlet's circumstances would not feel the heroic urge to see that justice is done. In short, what Laertes, Fortinbras, and Horatio are and what they say or do help to define what Hamlet is: he is first of all someone different from them. Of course the remaining characters—most notably Polonius, Gertrude, and especially Claudius, with whom Hamlet in effect is at war—also play a part in defining Hamlet's character.

Now, though character and plot are different things, in practice they are often inseparable. As Henry James rhetorically asked, "What is character but the determination of incident? What is incident but the illustration of character?" In the tragedies especially we feel that character determines plot, but even in the comedies, where a sense of chance is stronger, character and plot are connected, chance seeming to favor the virtuous. Shakespeare's plots are commonly organized so that scenes modify one another; thus the events, to apply Bottom's words, "grow to a point." For the Elizabethans, the "plot" was the groundplan of a play, a list of scenes posted backstage so that the actors could know when they would next be needed. In this sense, "plot" is to be distinguished from "story," which is simply the gist of the narrative; thus all plays about, say, the death of Julius Caesar tell pretty much the same story, as do the history books. But a plot is the choice and arrangement of episodes. The first scene of Shakespeare's *Julius Caesar,* showing the tribunes rebuking the citizens, is not a necessary part of the story of Caesar's fall, but it is a part of Shakespeare's plot, for it introduces the motifs of hostility to Caesar, the mob's fickleness, and (illustrated by the fall of Pompey) the transience of power. Thus the oft-repeated notion that Shakespeare borrowed all his plots is false. He borrowed his stories, and arranged them into his own plots, selecting episodes and linking them into meaningful relationships. For example, like the first scene of *Julius Caesar,* the first scene of *Hamlet* is not essential to the story. Indeed, the talk about a possible war between Denmark and Norway proves to be a red herring, for no such war develops; and the Ghost reappears in Hamlet's presence, so it need not appear now. What function, then, does this scene have in the plot? Quite practically, of course, it gets the audience quiet before the main characters appear. In addition, the talk about the possibility of a war between Denmark and Norway introduces the web of doubt that stretches throughout the play, giving a sense of—and this is what *Hamlet* is partly about—the difficulty of meaningful action in a world of uncertainty. Finally, the first appearance of the Ghost (I.i) makes us see everything in the following scene with a double vision. We listen to the assembled court, but we listen to it with a knowledge that none of the courtiers has. Thus, for example, we not only sense Hamlet's numbness when he speaks of the "weary, stale, flat, and unprofitable" world; we also know, as he does not, that a spiritual principle is active in it.

In short, each scene adds an increment to the story, but each scene also modifies all that has come before it, developing our understanding of what is happening and our understanding of the characters. As the example from *Hamlet* shows, a scene that appears to be unnecessary may contribute to the point; one is almost tempted to say that in Shakespeare when something seems to be unnecessary and therefore unimportant it must be very important. *Macbeth* provides another example. When Macduff and Malcolm are at the English court (IV.iii), the action seems to stop. But this scene has several important functions: (1) Malcolm's suspicion of Macduff shows the enormous suspicion that Macbeth's tyranny has engendered; (2) Malcolm's dissembling is for a good purpose, in contrast to Macbeth's, which is for a wicked purpose; (3) Malcolm's enumeration of "the king-becoming graces," such as "justice, verity, temp'rance, stableness," tells us what Macbeth lacks; (4) the English king's miraculous healing of the sick suggests that a rightful king has a divine power that makes his country wholesome, whereas Macbeth, a usurper, has brought "disease" to Scotland (V.iii.50–52); (5) the setting in England adds breadth to the play and suggests the infusion of new forces, which are made explicit at the end of the scene, with "the pow'rs above/Put on their instruments."

The interrelationships between stories can also be seen in *A Midsummer Night's Dream,* which is much more complicated in plot than *Macbeth.* There is the story of Theseus and Hippolyta, who will be married in four days; the story of the four young lovers; the story of Bottom and his fellow craftsmen, who are rehearsing a play; and the story of the quarreling fairies. All these stories are related, and eventually come together: the lovers marry on the same day as Theseus and Hippolyta; the craftsmen perform their play at the wedding; the fairies come to witness the wedding and bless it. One of the play's themes, of course, is love, as shown in the contrasts between the stately love of Theseus and Hippolyta, the changeable romantic love of the four young Athenians, the love of Pyramus and Thisby in the play that the craftsmen are rehearsing, the quarrel between the fairy king and queen, and even Titania's infatuation with Bottom. All these stories play against one another, sometimes very subtly, and sometimes explicitly, as when Lysander, having shifted his affection from Hermia to Helena, says, "Reason says you are the worthier maid" (II.ii.116), and Bottom in the next scene accepts Titania's love, saying, "Reason and love keep little company together nowadays" (III.i.142–43). The nature of reason is also implicitly discussed in the play, in the numerous references to "fantasy" and "fancy," or imagination. There is scarcely a scene that does not touch on the matter of the power of the imagination. In the opening scene, for example, Egeus says that Lysander has corrupted Hermia's fantasy (I.i.32), and Duke Theseus tells Hermia that she must perceive her suitors as her father perceives them. The most famous of these references is Theseus' speech on "the lunatic, the lover, and the poet" (V.1.7). In addition to setting the time and place, the images help to define the nature of fantasy: there is an emphasis on night and moonlight during the period of confusion, and then references to the "morning lark," "day," and so on, when Theseus (the spokesman for reason) enters the woods and the lovers are properly paired (IV.i.104 ff.). The last scene reintroduces night, and the lovers have moved from the dark wood back to the civilized world of Athens, and the night will bring them to bed. The plot of *A Midsummer Night's Dream*, then, juxtaposes speech against speech, image against image, and scene against scene, telling not simply a story but a story that "grows to something of great constancy, . . . strange and admirable."

6

A Note on Shakespeare's English

PRONUNCIATION, ACCENTS, PUNS

From the philologist's point of view at least, Shakespeare's English is Modern English. It requires footnotes, but the inexperienced reader can often comprehend a substantial passage with very little help; on the other hand, for the same reader Middle English is a foreign language. By the beginning of the fifteenth century the chief grammatical changes in English had taken place, and the final unaccented *-e* of Middle English had been lost (though it survives even today in spelling, as in *name*); during the fifteenth century the dialect of London, the commercial and political center, gradually displaced the provincial dialects, at least in writing; by the end of the century, printing helped to regularize and stabilize the language, especially spelling. Elizabethan spelling may seem erratic to us (there were dozens of spellings of *Shakespeare*, and a simple word like *been* was also spelled *beene* or *bin*), but it had much in common with our own spelling. Elizabethan spelling was conservative in that for the most part it reflected an older pronunciation (Middle English) rather than the sound of the language as it was then spoken, just as our spelling continues to reflect medieval pronunciation—most obviously in the now-silent letters in a word such as *knight*. Elizabethan pronunciation, though not identical with ours, was closer to ours than to that of the Middle Ages.

There are three areas in which an awareness of the difference between our pronunciation and Shakespeare's is crucial: in accent, or number of syllables (many metrically regular lines may look irregular to us); in rhymes; and in puns (which may not look like puns to us). Examples may be useful here. Some words that were at least on occasion stressed differently from today are *aspéct, cómplete, revénue,* and *sepúlcher.* Words that sometimes had an additional syllable are *emp[e]ress, Hen-[e]ry, món[e]th,* and *villain;* words that had one less syllable than now are *needle* (pronounced "neel") and *violet.* Among rhymes now lost are *one* with *loan, love* with *prove, beast* with *jest, eat* with *great.* An example of a pun that has become obliterated by a change in pronunciation is Falstaff's reply to Prince Hal's "Come, tell us your reason" in *1 Henry IV*: "Give you a reason on compulsion? If reasons were as plentiful as blackberries, I would give no man a reason upon compulsion, I" (II.iv.239–42). The *ea* in *reason* was pronounced rather like a long *a,* like the *ai* in *raisin;* hence the comparison with blackberries.

Puns, of course, are not merely attempts to be funny; like metaphors, they often involve bringing into a meaningful relationship areas of experience normally seen as remote. In *2 Henry IV,* III.ii.239–40, when Feeble is conscripted, he stoically says, "I care not. A man can die but once. We owe God a death," punning on *debt,* which was the way *death* was pronounced. Here an enormously significant fact of life is put into simple commercial imagery, suggesting its commonplace quality. Shakespeare used the same pun earlier in *1 Henry IV,* V.i.126, when Prince Hal says to Falstaff, "Why, thou owest God a death," and Falstaff wittily replies, " 'Tis not due yet: I would be loath to pay him before his day. What need I be so forward with him that calls not on me?" Sometimes the puns reveal a delightful playfulness; sometimes they reveal aggressiveness, as when Hamlet replies to Claudius' "But now, my cousin Hamlet, and my son" with "A little more than kin, and less than kind!" (I.ii.65). These are Hamlet's first words in the play, and we already hear him warring verbally against Claudius. Hamlet's "less than kind" probably means (1) Hamlet is not of Claudius' family or nature, "kind" having the sense it still has in our word "mankind"; (2) Hamlet is not.

kindly (affectionately) disposed toward Claudius; (3) Claudius is not naturally (but rather unnaturally, incestuously) Hamlet's father. The puns, evidently, were not put in as sops to the groundlings; they are an important way of communicating a complex meaning.

VOCABULARY

A conspicuous difficulty in reading Shakespeare is the fact that some of his words are no longer in common use—for example, words concerned with armor, astrology, clothing, coinage, hawking, horsemanship, law, medicine, sailing, and war. Shakespeare had an immense vocabulary—something between twenty-thousand and thirty-thousand words—but it was not so much a vocabulary of big or learned words as a vocabulary drawn from a wide range of life, and it is partly his ability to call upon a great body of concrete language that gives his plays the sense of being in close contact with life. (When the right word did not already exist, he made it up. Among his numerous coinages apparently are the following: *accommodation, all-knowing, amazement, barefaced, dexterously, dislocate, excitement, fancy-free, frugal, indistinguishable, lackluster, obscene, overawe, premeditated, seachange, star-crossed, submerge.* Among those that have not survived are the words *convive,* meaning feast together, and *smilet,* a little smile.)

Less overtly troublesome than the technical words but more treacherous are the words that seem readily intelligible to us but whose Elizabethan meanings are not identical with their modern meanings. When Horatio describes the Ghost as an "erring spirit," he is saying not that the ghost has sinned or made an error but that it is wandering. Here is a short list of some of the most common words in Shakespeare's plays that often (but not always) have a meaning other than their most usual modern meaning:

'a he; *abuse* deceive; *accident* occurrence; *advertise* inform; *an, and* if; *annoy* harm; *appeal* accuse; *artificial* skillful; *brave* fine, splen-

did; *censure* opinion; *cheer* (1) face (2) frame of mind; *chorus* a single person who comments on the events; *closet* small private room; *competitor* partner; *conceit* idea, imagination; *cousin* kinsman; *cunning* skillful; *disaster* evil astrological influence; *doom* judgment; *entertain* receive into service; *envy* malice; *event* outcome; *excrement* outgrowth (of hair); *fact* evil deed; *fancy* (1) love (2) imagination; *fell* cruel; *fellow* (1) companion (2) low person (often an insulting term if addressed to someone of approximately equal rank); *fond* foolish; *free* (1) innocent (2) liberal, generous; *glass* mirror; *hap, haply* chance, by chance; *head* army; *humor* (1) mood (2) bodily fluid; *imp* child; *intelligence* news; *kind* natural, acting according to nature; *let* hinder; *lewd* base; *mere(ly)* utter(ly); *modern* commonplace; *natural* a fool or an idiot; *naughty* (1) wicked (2) worthless; *next* nearest; *nice* (1) trivial (2) fussy; *noise* music; *policy* (1) prudence (2) stratagem; *presently* immediately; *prevent* anticipate; *prove* test; *quick* alive; *sad* serious; *saw* proverb; *secure* without care, incautious; *silly* innocent; *sensible* capable of being perceived by the senses; *shrewd* sharp; *so* provided that; *starve* die; *still* always; *success* that which follows; *tall* brave; *tell* count; *tonight* last night; *wanton* playful, careless; *watch* keep awake; *will* lust; *wink* close both eyes; *wit* mind, intelligence.

All glosses, of course, are mere approximations; sometimes one of Shakespeare's words may hover between an older meaning and a modern one, and as has been seen, his words often have multiple meanings.

ELLIPSIS, TRANSFERRED EPITHET, HENDIADYS

Ellipsis, or the omission of words that are assumed to be understood, also causes difficulty occasionally, but most often it does not, as in "And he to England shall along with you," where "go" is understood. When read aloud an elliptical line often becomes clear. Other sources of slight difficulty are transferred epithets, as in "idle bed" for "bed of idleness," where "idle" is transferred from the person to the bed, and hendiadys, or the use of two nouns joined by a conjunction instead of a noun and a modifier, as in "with every gale and vary" for "with every varying gale" and "this . . . gentleness and course" for "this . . . gentle course."

GRAMMAR

A few matters of grammar may be surveyed, though it should be noted at the outset that because Shakespeare was a poet he sometimes made up his own grammar. As E. A. Abbott says in *A Shakespearian Grammar,* almost any part of speech can be used as any other part of speech: a noun as a verb ("He childed as I fathered"); a verb as a noun ("She hath made compare"); or an adverb as an adjective ("a seldom pleasure"). There are hundreds, perhaps thousands, of such instances in Shakespeare's plays, many of which at first glance would not seem at all irregular and would trouble only a pedant. But here are a few broad matters. The Elizabethans thought that the –s genitive ending for *nouns* (as in *man's*) derived from *his;* thus the line " 'Gainst the count his galleys I did some service" for "the count's galleys." By Shakespeare's time *adjectives* had lost the endings that once indicated gender, number, and case. About the only difference between Shakespeare's adjectives and ours is the use of the now-redundant *more* or *most* with the comparative or superlative: "This was the most unkindest cut of all." (Like double comparatives and double superlatives, double negatives were acceptable: Mercutio "will not budge for no man's pleasure.") The greatest change was in *pronouns.* In Middle English the singular forms *thou, thy,* and *thee* were used among familiars and in speaking to children and inferiors; the plural forms *ye, your,* and *you* were used in speaking to a superior or to an equal with whom one was not familiar. Increasingly the "polite" forms were used in all direct address, regardless of rank, and the accusative *you* displaced the nominative *ye.* Shakespeare sometimes uses *ye* instead of *you,* but even in Shakespeare's day *ye* was archaic, and it occurs mostly in rhetorical appeals. *Thou, thy,* and *thee* were not completely displaced, however, and Shakespeare occasionally makes significant use of them, sometimes to connote familiarity or intimacy and sometimes to connote contempt. In *Twelfth Night* Sir Toby advises Sir Andrew to insult Cesario by addressing him as *thou*: "If thou thou'st him some thrice, it shall not be amiss" (III.ii.44). In *Othello* when Brabantio is addressing an unidentified voice in the dark he says, "What are you?" (I.i.91), but when the voice identifies itself as the foolish suitor Roderigo, Brabantio uses the contemptuous form, saying in line 93, "I have charged thee not to haunt about my doors." He uses this form for a while, but later in the scene, when he comes to regard Roderigo as an ally, he shifts again to the polite *you,* beginning in line 163: "What said she to you?" and so on to the end of the scene. Perhaps the most unusual use of pronouns, from our point of view, is the neuter singular. *His* was often used in place of our *its,* as in "How far that little candle throws *his* beams." But the use of a masculine pronoun for a neuter noun came to seem unnatural, and so *it* was used for the possessive as well as the nominative: "The hedge-sparrow fed the cuckoo so long/That it had it head bit off by it young." (In the late sixteenth century the possessive form *its* apparently developed by analogy with the *–s* ending used to indicate a genitive noun, as in *book's.* But *its* was not yet common usage in Shakespeare's day. It has been said that Shakespeare uses *its* only ten times, mostly in his later plays.) Other usages, such as "You have seen Cassio and she together" or the substitution of *who* for *whom,* cause no difficulty even when noticed. *Verbs* too cause almost no difficulty: the third person singular present form commonly ends in *–s,* as in Modern English, but sometimes it ends in *–eth* (Portia explains to Shylock that mercy "blesseth him that gives and him that takes"). Broadly speaking, *–eth* was old-fashioned or dignified or "literary" rather than colloquial, except for the words *doth, hath,* and *saith.* The *–eth* ending (regularly used in the King James Bible, 1611) is very rare in Shakespeare's dramatic prose, though not surprisingly it occurs twice in the rather formal prose summary of the narrative poem *Lucrece.* Sometimes a plural subject, especially if it has collective force, takes a verb ending in *–s,* as in "My old bones aches." Some of our strong or irregular preterites (such as *broke*) have a different form in Shakespeare (*brake*); some verbs that now have a weak or regular preterite (such as *helped*) in Shakespeare have a strong or irregular preterite (*holp*). Some *adverbs* that today end in *–ly* were not inflected: "grievous sick," "wondrous strange." Finally, *prepositions* often are not the ones we expect: "We are such stuff as dreams are made on"; "I have a king here to my flatterer."

Again, none of these differences (except meanings that have substantially changed or been lost) causes much difficulty. But it must be confessed that for some elliptical passages there is no widespread agreement on meaning. Wise editors resist saying more than they know, and when they are uncertain they add a question mark to their gloss, inviting the reader to think of a better interpretation.

Part Two

THE WORKS

First, a brief disclaimer. The following survey separates the plays into the three divisions established by the First Folio (1623): Comedies, Histories, Tragedies. It thus somewhat obscures the connections that all of the plays share, whatever their genre. For example, it obscures the fact that love, one of the chief concerns of the comedies, is also explored in such tragedies as *Hamlet* and *King Lear* (to say nothing of *Romeo and Juliet, Othello,* and *Antony and Cleopatra*); consider, for example, Hamlet's scenes with Ophelia and with his mother and even with Horatio and Rosencrantz and Guildenstern. The history plays, too, would be relevant; we remember Falstaff and Mistress Quickly, Hotspur and Lady Percy. And when we remember Hotspur's unwillingness to share his plans with his wife, we may recall that a few years later Shakespeare's Brutus similarly will not reveal his mind to his wife Portia, and that a few years still later Macbeth will not tell Lady Macbeth of his plan to kill Banquo. Yet to pursue all such connections one would have to be the medieval hero who leaped onto his horse and rode off in all directions. A less ambitious activity is followed here.

7

The Comedies

The First Folio edition of Shakespeare's plays prints fourteen works under the heading "Comedies"; to these we can add *Cymbeline*, printed with the tragedies, and two plays absent from the Folio, *Pericles* and *The Two Noble Kinsmen*. Some editors add an eighteenth play, *Troilus and Cressida* (here discussed with the tragedies), printed in the Folio in unnamed territory between the histories and the tragedies.

If we look at Shakespearean comedy as a whole (and overlook a good deal) we see that generally speaking it is a comedy in which illusions, whether based on chance, self-deception, or trickery, are happily dispelled. The story line commonly involves young lovers who encounter difficulties but who are ultimately united. The plays thus follow the Renaissance formula for comedy; according to Shakespeare's fellow playwright Thomas Heywood, "comedies begin in trouble and end in peace." Thus, in the first act of *A Midsummer Night's Dream*, Egeus appears:

> Full of vexation come I, with complaint
> Against my child, my daughter Hermia. (I.i.22–23)

Egeus wants Hermia to marry Demetrius, but she is in love with Lysander, and so Egeus calls upon the law, which holds that she must follow her father's will or suffer either death or life in a cloister. The play ends with Hermia marrying her beloved Lysander, Demetrius marrying a girl who dotes upon him, and a few other happy bits. In the words of Puck, who quotes "the country proverb":

> Jack shall have Jill;
> Nought shall go ill;
> The man shall have his mare again, and all shall be well.
>   (III.ii.461–63)

Similarly, at the start of *The Merchant of Venice* Antonio is mysteriously troubled, Bassanio is in financial difficulties, and Portia is unpleasantly confined by the terms of her father's will. At the end of the play all these problems are solved. The heroines of the comedies are liberated, and the plays regularly end with marriage:

> Wedding is great Juno's crown,
>   O blessed bond of board and bed!
> 'Tis Hymen peoples every town;
>   High wedlock then be honorèd.
> Honor, high honor, and renown
> To Hymen, god of every town!   (*As You Like It*, V.iv.141–46)

As Northrop Frye has pointed out, Shakespeare often contrasts two worlds, not merely a world of age against a world of youth but an urban, troubled world against a more pastoral world, which Frye calls "the green world." In this world characters undergo a renewal and find what they are seeking: *A Midsummer Night's Dream* begins in Athens, the place of the quarrel between Egeus and his daughter, then moves into the moonlit forest, where wonderful transformations occur, and finally returns to Athens, which is no longer a place "full of vexation" but a "blessed" place full of "jollity." In *The Merchant of Venice* too there is a contrast (not in all details, but a contrast nevertheless) between Venice, the home of the unpleasant Shylock, and Belmont, Portia's estate, a place of music, beauty, and wooing. Like the woods outside Athens, Belmont is sometimes said to be moonlit. In *The Merchant of Venice* there is no final return to the urban world; but in those plays where there is such a return, the urban or "real" world seems to be transformed by the infusion from the green or "ideal" world. Corresponding to the renewal of society is the renewal of the individual; the individual usually finds what he wants and in doing so sometimes finds that he is freed from a misapprehension or constricting view. Thus at the end of *The Taming of the Shrew* Katherine discovers that she does not really wish to dominate men; at the end of *As You Like It* Duke Frederick and Oliver, finding that they do not wish to tyrannize good men, reform. Put generally, the characters are subjected to trying circumstances and at the end emerge with enriched personalities.

Broadly speaking (and allowance must be made for important exceptions), Shakespeare's comedies are romantic, evocative of wonder or amazement as well as of amusement. They tell of the trials and the ultimate successes in love of aristocratic young people. Behind them are earlier Renaissance plays of courtship, adventure, wandering, and reunion, and behind these in turn is the medieval idea of the power of love to conquer and transform. In 1582 Stephen Gosson, a hostile critic of drama, irritably characterized the romantic plays of his age: "Sometime you shall see nothing but the adventures of an amorous knight, passing from country to country for the love of his lady, encountering many a terrible monster of brown paper. . . . What learn you by that? When the soul of your plays is either mere trifles, or Italian bawdry, or wooing of gentlewomen, what are we taught?" In *A Midsummer Night's Dream* Shakespeare himself affectionately alludes to the taste that wanted "the adventures of an amorous knight" when Francis Flute, a bellows mender, wonders if his part in the amateur theatrical will be "a wand'ring knight."

If we divide comedy into two sorts, romantic comedy (showing a dreamlike world of delightful lovers) and satiric comedy (showing a world of people who behave as we ought not to behave), Shakespeare's comedies, despite some satire of romance, belong to the former group. By Shakespeare's time, romantic plots—at least when handled by the better dramatists —were no longer the mere episodic adventures they had been in the seventies: daring fights against monsters of brown paper had been eliminated, but wooing continued, and the spirit of fun, surprise, and adventure remained. Shakespeare's slightly later contemporary, Ben Jonson, who preferred satiric comedy, compared romantic to satiric comedy in *Every Man Out of His Humor.* Jonson's first speaker prefers romantic comedy and rejects comedy that is "near and familiarly allied to the time," but the second speaker puts him in his place, rejecting the stuff of the popular stage and citing instead an ancient authority:

MITIS The argument of his comedy might have been of some other nature, as of a duke to be in love with a countess, and that countess to be in love with the duke's son, and the son to love the lady's wait-ing-maid: some such cross-wooing, with a clown to their serving man, better than to be thus near and familiarly allied to the time.

CORDATUS You say well, but I would fain hear one of these autumn-judgments define once, *Quid sit comoedia* [what is comedy]? If he cannot, let him content himself with Cicero's definition (till he have strength to propose to himself a better) who would have a comedy to be *Imitatio vitae, speculum consuetudinis, imago veritatis* [an imitation of life, a mirror of customs, the image of truth]; a thing throughout pleasant and ridiculous, and accommodated to the cor-rection of manners.

Jonson is one with Gosson here, in the assumption that com-edy should teach. His hostile description of what seemed to him a pointless chain of lovers is almost a description of Shakespeare's *Twelfth Night,* in which Orsino is in love with Olivia, Olivia is in love with Cesario (really Viola disguised as a boy), and Cesario-Viola is in love with Orsino. (There is no serving man who is a clown, but there is a clown.) Of course, within the romance there is occasional satire—satire not only of crabby impediments to love but even of love itself; yet curiously we do not think the less of the lovers for seeing their faults. When the heroine of *As You Like It,* Rosalind, disguised as a boy, learns that her beloved Orlando is nearby, she says:

Alas the day! What shall I do with my doublet and hose? What did he when thou saw'st him? What said he? How looked he? Wherein went he? What makes he here? Did he ask for me? Where remains he? How parted he with thee? And when shalt thou see him again? Answer me in one word.   (III.ii.220–25)

If we laugh *at* her, however, we also laugh *with* her, delighting in her wit, her gaiety, and her resourcefulness, all of which (clearly in evidence in other parts of the play when she herself mocks at love) suggest a golden world in contrast to the brazen world of satiric comedy. But this vision of a golden world in Shakespeare's comedies in a way relates the comedies to satiric comedy, for the golden world is a reminder that our own lives are less lovely than we like to think they are. We glimpse a better world, "rich and strange," "strange and admirable," an implicit criticism of what we take to be normal life.

When Rosalind leaves the court for the Forest of Arden, she goes to a place where "merry men . . . live like the old Robin Hood of England. They say many young gentlemen . . . fleet the time carelessly as they did in the golden world" (I.i.113–117). The evocation of Robin Hood, the emphasis upon a joyous ("care-less") existence, and the reference to a golden world (Northrop Frye's "green world") suggest a life of harmonious play and a spirit of fun. Indeed, something of a holiday spirit is suggested by the very names of some of the comedies: *A Midsummer Night's Dream, Much Ado About Nothing, As You Like It,* and *Twelfth Night, or What You Will.* The festive spirit is present everywhere, even in moments of strain. When Rosalind says, in *As You Like It,* "How full of briers is this working-day world," Celia replies, "They are but burrs, cousin, thrown upon thee in holiday foolery (I.iii.12–14). Festivity is of course especially evident at the end of a comedy, when all has been set right, and it sometimes extends even to the spoilsport who represents a threat to happiness in the earlier parts of the play. At the end of *The Merry Wives of Windsor,* for example, Sir John Falstaff, who has been humiliated by the two women he had sought to seduce, is invited to join in the fun, and even the jealous husband Ford agrees:

> let us every one go home,
> And laugh this sport o'er by a country fire;
> Sir John and all.

FORD   Let it be so.   (V.v.240–42)

Like the characters in the play, the members of the audience richly enjoy themselves and return, vivified, from the world of "holiday foolery" to the "working-day world." In its spirit, Shakespearean comedy is thus close to the medieval folk plays performed at holiday time that concluded with a sense of renewal (see p. 30). It does not teach us in the way that Gosson thought comedy should teach, but its imaginative worlds surely exhibit joyful new possibilities that evoke a sense of wonder to which we offer willing assent.

If Shakespearean comedy is indebted for much of its spirit to festive rites, it is indebted for some of its shape to the Roman comedy of Plautus (254?–184 B.C.) and Terence (190?–159? B.C.), which itself was indebted to the New Comedy of Greece. Old Comedy, represented by Aristophanes, though phallic and ending in a *komos*, or celebration of sexual union, was primarily satirical and political. New Comedy, represented by Menander (343?–291? B.C.) was of the boy-meets-girl sort, though it was not romantic by our standards because it dealt more with sex and seduction than with love. In this type of comedy a young man wants a girl—often a slave girl—and with the aid of a clever slave outwits the pander who owns her and who sometimes plans to sell her to someone less attractive than the hero. In *The Taming of the Shrew* Grumio sums it up: "See, to beguile the old folks, how the young folks lay their heads together" (I.ii.137–38). Terence especially was much studied in Elizabethan schools, and he gave the Elizabethan dramatists—often at second or third hand—a sense of how to organize a plot. The late medieval cycle plays, which spanned time from the Creation through the Fall to the Last Judgment, established an episodic tradition, and this tradition, along with the medieval chivalric romances that were the sources of much romantic drama, makes most of the plays before the 1580's seem shapeless. But as the sixteenth century wore on, the professional drama became better established and came under the influence of men with considerable secular education. Had they had their way, some of these men would have turned the drama into lifeless imitations of ancient drama, and we can rejoice that the academic influence was never very great. But Roman and Italian plots helped to show dramatists how a story might be organized. Theoreticians studying Terence developed the idea that a play has a five-act structure: in the first act there is a situation with tensions; in the second the conflict that is implicit in the first is developed; in the third the conflict is open, reaches a height, and seems to arrive at an impasse; in the fourth act things begin to clear up, and in the fifth act all knots are untied. Few if any of the English popular playwrights felt obliged to follow this formula, but the best playwrights probably did think in terms of an overall plot rather than a series of episodes. There is little that is obviously Plautine or Terentian about Shakespeare's best comedies, but this is not to say that he learned nothing from these Roman playwrights. It is quite evident from *The Comedy of Errors,* which may have been Shakespeare's first play, that he learned a good deal, though he always transformed what he learned into something quite his own.

THE THREE EARLIEST COMEDIES:
THE COMEDY OF ERRORS,
THE TAMING OF THE SHREW,
THE TWO GENTLEMEN OF VERONA

It seems likely enough that Shakespeare began his career as a playwright—perhaps even before he went to London—by writing a play that closely resembles the Latin dramas that he would have read and perhaps acted in while in grammar school. *The Comedy of Errors,* though certainly more than an adaptation of Plautus, remains greatly indebted to Plautus' *Menaechmi,* a play about twins separated for most of their lives who after several episodes of mistaken identity at last meet and are reunited. Although the setting is bourgeois (an unusual setting for Shakespeare), there is a touch of romance, notably in a passage in which Antipholus of Syracuse woos Luciana:

> Sweet mistress, what your name is else, I know not;
> Nor by what wonder you do hit of mine;

> Less in your knowledge and your grace you show not
> Than our earth's wonder, more than earth divine.
> Teach me, dear creature, how to think and speak:
> Lay open to my earthy-gross conceit,
> Smoth'red in errors, feeble, shallow, weak,
> The folded meaning of your words' deceit.
> Against my soul's pure truth why labor you
> To make it wander in an unknown field?
> Are you a god? Would you create me new?
> Transform me, then, and to your pow'r I'll yield.   (III.ii.29–40)

The notion that a woman is godlike and can transform a man is nothing that Plautus or any other Roman comic dramatist would have thought of. Indeed, Luciana is Shakespeare's addition to Plautus' plot, an addition that enabled Shakespeare to end his play not merely with a family reunion but with the promise of a wedding.

Another important addition to Plautus is found in the first and last scenes concerning Egeon, the father of the twins. In *The Menaechmi* the father is dead; and when fathers do appear in classical comedy, they are outwitted, or at least laughed at. Drawing on the pseudo-Greek romance *Apollonius of Tyre,* which he was to use again late in his career in *Pericles,* Shakespeare began the play with a serious treatment of a despairing father sentenced to death, and concluded with the restoration of the father to his wife and children. The unanticipated appearance of the wife, who during the long separation has been an abbess, adds a hint of the miraculous or providential that is so evident in the later comedies, where it is often associated with rebirth or renewal involving the discovery of an enriched self. The motif of renewal consequent upon passing through traumatic situations is prepared for early in the play, when Antipholus of Syracuse says that as a lonely wanderer searching for his brother and mother he has lost his identity:

> I to the world am like a drop of water
> That in the ocean seeks another drop,
> Who, falling there to find his fellow forth,
> Unseen, inquisitive, confounds [loses] himself.

So I, to find a mother and a brother,
In quest of them, unhappy, lose myself. (I.ii.35–40)

The abundant subsequent references to witchcraft, which was believed to rob a man of his identity, continue the idea. In the fifth act the members of the family find each other and renew themselves, gaining a new life and a new sense of identity; this renewal is heightened for Antipholus of Syracuse, who is not only reunited with his family but also finds a woman who will become his wife. The sense of new identity appears also (as in Plautus) in the freeing of the slave, Dromio of Ephesus. (At the end of his career Shakespeare again uses this classical convention in *The Tempest* when Prospero frees Ariel.)

If there are great differences between *The Menaechmi* and Shakespeare's play, then, there are also numerous similarities. But even the similarities are with a difference. Dr. Pinch, for example, is derived from the stock classical character of the *medicus,* but he is thoroughly Elizabethan: "a mountebank, a threadbare juggler and a fortuneteller." It is characteristic of Shakespeare to make his borrowings his own, and if some of his plays have such stock figures as the *senex,* or old father —Egeus in *A Midsummer Night's Dream* or Shylock in *The Merchant of Venice*—the *adulescens,* or young lover, the *servus,* or servant, and so on, the characters are nevertheless transformed almost beyond recognition.

Finally, there is a pervasive difference in moral tone between the two plays. Shakespeare's play has bawdry, but the moral tone is notably higher than that of *The Menaechmi.* For example, Antipholus of Ephesus visits the Courtesan only after his wife bars him from his home, and Antipholus of Syracuse offers to pay for the gold chain that the Merchant gives to him. In short, although *The Comedy of Errors* is in obvious ways close to its source, it is indisputably a very different play from its source, and with hindsight we can see in it some of the directions that Shakespeare was to take in later and greater plays.

There is a good deal of uncertainty about whether Shake-

speare's *The Taming of the Shrew* is based on an earlier
comedy, but it is clear that the chief plot of the play—"the
taming of the shrew"—is derived ultimately from a widespread bit of folklore. To this Shakespeare added the story of
Bianca and her suitors, derived from Italian Renaissance
comedy, with its intriguing servant (here Tranio), its outwitted old men, and its trio of suitors. The setting is bourgeois,
as in only two of Shakespeare's other comedies, *The Comedy
of Errors* and *The Merry Wives of Windsor*; Petruchio sees
marriage chiefly as an economic institution ("I come to wive
it wealthily in Padua"), and although we may at first think
that the Lucentio-Bianca plot is more romantic (the two young
people fall in love at first sight), the play is not yet the sort
of romantic comedy that Shakespeare was to write at the turn
of the century in *The Merchant of Venice, Much Ado About
Nothing, As You Like It,* and *Twelfth Night.* But this is not
to say *The Taming of the Shrew* is a failure because it is not
romantic; one of its chief delights is the fact that the romantic
marriage of Bianca and Lucentio at the end dwindles into
bickering, while the marriage of Petruchio and Katherine
turns out to be (at least in sixteenth-century terms) mutually
satisfactory. There is, after all, much to be said for—and much
to delight in—the realistic view uttered by Petruchio's servant: "Winter tames man, woman, and beast; for it hath tamed
my old master, and my new mistress, and myself" (IV.i.20–22).
Seen thus, the taming of the shrew is not brutality but a
schooling in humanity. Although Petruchio tames Katherine
by humiliating her, in one important motif the play looks
forward to the later comedies: he tames her by pretending
that she is not shrewish but "pleasant, gamesome, passing
courteous" (II.i.239). Indeed, such is the power of the lover's
imagination that the beloved is subsequently freed from the
"mad and headstrong" tantrums that possess her and is transformed into Petruchio's image. She is, one can say, cured of
her crippling, self-indulgent personality. Early in the play
(II.i), during the course of her schooling, Katherine becomes
sufficiently sensitized to protest against Petruchio's treatment
of the Tailor and the Haberdasher, and finally she becomes

an ideal wife. Having shaken off a constricting personality, she at last assumes her proper role in society. This theme of a change in personality, the formation of a new identity— already treated in *The Comedy of Errors*—has a comic parallel in the Induction, where Christopher Sly, a drunken tinker, is persuaded when he awakens from his stupor that he is a lord who for fifteen years has been mentally ill. Sly even changes his language for a while from prose to blank verse. This part of the play ends inconclusively with a few lines between I.i and I.ii in which Sly continues to play the lord. His transformation cannot have the permanence of Katherine's, since romantic comedy shows moral rather than social or economic change. Perhaps there was originally an Epilogue, now lost, in which Sly resumes his workaday character (in *A Midsummer Night's Dream* Bottom is similarly transformed and "translated" back again without difficulty).

The Two Gentlemen of Verona approaches what was to become Shakespeare's characteristic comedy: the heart of the plot, derived from a chivalric and pastoral tale, is the story of courtly lovers who, in a romantic environment, engage in what has been called an obstacle race to the altar. The relationship between love and friendship is explored, and although the lovers are not yet very interesting, the appearance of a heroine disguised as a boy suggests the world of the romantic comedies, which (in words from *Twelfth Night*) "give a very echo to the seat/Where love is throned." Of particular interest is the spoofing of love, which in the later comedies (and in *Romeo and Juliet*) helps to define love. After listening to a conversation between Valentine and Silvia, Speed comments: "Though the chameleon love can feed on the air, I am one that am nourished by my victuals, and would fain have meat" (II.i.171–73). To help show both the folly of love and the difference between courtly love and clownish love, there is a clown in love. Thinking of his beloved's virtues, the clown Launce says, "She can fetch and carry. Why, a horse can do no more: nay, a horse cannot fetch, but only carry; therefore is she better than a jade" (III.i.274–76).

Moreover, although there is an evident delight in wordplay, especially in the puns of the clownish servants, speech in *Two Gentlemen* is more closely related to character than in the earlier comedies. There are very few ornate set pieces that are almost detachable from the speakers—though we are grateful for the exquisite song "Who Is Silvia". and for Launce's comic monologue on his dog's indifference (II.iii), both of which are almost independent bits. (Launce's devotion to his dog can be justified as a parody of the theme of friendship, but it is not for the speech's thematic relevance that we value it.) The play also includes a host of motifs and devices that appear in later plays: a woman disguises herself as a boy, a man mistakenly trusts a false companion, the heroine and her lady-in-waiting discuss suitors (compare I.ii with *The Merchant of Venice*, I.ii), a lover is anatomized (compare II.i.19–33 with *As You Like It*, III.ii.371–81), and characters gather in a forest or wood and are converted, thus forming a better society at the end. This last point has been touched on earlier, but it is worth repeating that at the heart of some of Shakespeare's comedies is a "green world" where illusions are dissolved and where people form a regenerated society. This regenerated society is presumed to be stable, unlike the capricious, whimsical, and sometimes arbitrary and tyrannical society at the outset of the play, when lovers are inconstant or thwarted. In *The Two Gentlemen of Verona* the fickle Proteus, rightly characterized by his best friend as a "treacherous man," and characterized by more than one critic as a nincompoop, is presumably converted to constancy, and the play ends with "one feast, one house, one mutual happiness."

THE ACHIEVEMENT OF POETIC COMEDY: LOVE'S LABOR'S LOST

The date of *Love's Labor's Lost* is uncertain, and it is entirely possible that the only existing text is a revision, possibly as late as 1597, of a play that Shakespeare wrote as early as 1588. In its present form, although the plot is tenuous, the play has

a splendid poetry of a sort not found in Shakespeare's earlier
plays; probably the writing of his two long narrative poems,
Venus and Adonis (1593) and *The Rape of Lucrece* (1594),
and of some sonnets greatly assisted his development as a poet.
There are type-characters—Berowne speaks of "the pedant,
the braggart, the hedge-priest, the fool, and the boy"—and
Holofernes the pedant especially is infatuated with words and
with the "odoriferous flowers of fancy." But Shakespeare vi-
talizes the type-characters of the *commedia dell' arte* and he
masters the "taffeta phrases, silken terms precise," and the
"golden cadence," giving us so fine a dramatic speech as this:

KING
Let fame, that all hunt after in their lives,
Live regist'red upon our brazen tombs
And then grace us in the disgrace of death,
When, spite of cormorant devouring Time,
Th' endeavor of this present breath may buy
That honor which shall bate his scythe's keen edge
And make us heirs of all eternity.
Therefore, brave conquerors—for so you are
That war against your own affections
And the huge army of the world's desires—
Our late edict shall strongly stand in force:
Navarre shall be the wonder of the world;
Our court shall be a little academe,
Still and contemplative in living art.
You three, Berowne, Dumaine, and Longaville,
Have sworn for three years' term to live with me,
My fellow scholars, and to keep those statutes
That are recorded in this schedule here.
Your oaths are passed; and now subscribe your names,
That his own hand may strike his honor down
That violates the smallest branch herein.
If you are armed to do as sworn to do,
Subscribe to your deep oaths, and keep it too.   (I.i.1–23)

One might call attention to this speech as an expression of the
Renaissance awareness of the tragic brevity of life, and of the
Renaissance habit of trying to win glory by a great achieve-
ment so that at least one's reputation will survive devouring

Time. But the point to be made here is that the earlier Elizabethan stage had rarely heard such excellent dramatic poetry, and some of its dramatic excellence resides in the fact that these resounding lines somehow convey a hint that they are too facile, a hint that their speaker does not know enough about life. No less excellent is the prose. A few minutes after the courtiers sign a bond to study for three years and not "to see a woman in that term," the clown Costard is brought in by Constable Dull for having been caught with a wench. Costard explains: "It is the manner of a man to speak to a woman. . . . Such is the simplicity of man to hearken after the flesh" (I.i. 209–17). Thus the king's fine speech is clownishly put into its proper perspective. Costard can be generous as well as exact. Later in the play he comes to the defense of Nathaniel, who like a good Elizabethan has performed in an amateur theatrical to entertain his betters but has not been able to sustain his role of Alexander in the show of the Nine Worthies (heroes of history and legend):

There, an't shall please you, a foolish mild man; an honest man, look you, and soon dashed. He is a marvelous good neighbor, faith, and a very good bowler; but for Alisander—alas! you see how 'tis— a little o'erparted.   (V.ii.576–80)

One can regret the abundance of topical allusions in the play—more properly, one can regret that the allusions are now baffling—and perhaps we cannot fully enjoy a comedy that is largely based on the premise that inflated language is the sign of some sort of moral failure in the speaker. Perhaps, too, the wit occasionally overwhelms the action (one senses labor in the play as well as in the title), but the play is certainly not without action in the sense of a motive or theme, for it dramatizes the infirmity of idealism. Berowne early perceives the limits of idealism, remarking that "every man with his affects [passions] is born,/Not by might mastered, but by special grace" (I.i.150–51), and the truth of his perception becomes apparent, as we have seen, when Constable Dull brings in Costard. In mocking the high-minded courtiers who make war against their "own affections/And the huge army of the world's desires" (I.i.9–10), Shakespeare comes near to writing a satirical play, but there is something so noble in the courtiers' aspiration and something so delightful (and beautiful) in their absurdity that we do not view them with contempt. Satire diminishes the object of its attack; as Ezra Pound has said in *Literary Essays*, "Satire reminds one that certain things are not worthwhile. It draws one to consider time wasted." But in *Love's Labor's Lost* although we laugh at the courtiers, first for their efforts to forswear women and then for their efforts to win women, we also gain a glimpse of a world of delightful and high-minded rather than worthless people. We are pleased that when they finally are reconciled to the fact that "it is the manner of a man to speak to a woman" they are not crushed by their enlightenment; indeed, if we value life, we can scarcely regret that their idealism is displaced by a recognition of man's physical nature. Costard, after all, is on the side of life, as the courtiers come to see. But at the end of the play—and this is most unusual in Shakespeare's comedies—the young men are not allowed to marry the women they court. Berowne complains, "Our wooing doth not end like an old play;/Jack hath not Jill," and remarkably the last words are not about union or reunion but about separation: "You that way, we this way." The later comedies conclude more harmoniously, with the journey ending in lovers meeting, but these comedies also sometimes include a touch of melancholy or disharmony. For example, Jaques in *As You Like It* and Malvolio in *Twelfth Night* stand apart from the happiness that dominates the final scenes, complicating the vision of the play. In *Love's Labor's Lost,* the happiness that the courtiers project in their dream of an academe is dispelled, and later the happiness that they project in their roles as lovers is also dispelled by the announcement that the princess' father has died. The weddings must be postponed for a year, during which time the men must do penance imposed by the ladies. (The women in Shakespeare's comedies are often a good deal wiser than the men. In *Love's Labor's Lost,* for example, the women are no less witty than the men but they know that wit is not the whole of life, and they see that in the men wit is often a cruel affectation. Berowne comes to see that women are better teachers than books: "They are the ground, the books, the academes,/From whence doth spring the true Promethean fire" [IV.iii.300–01]). But the ending is not merely melancholy, for the implications are that the recognition of the reality of death and the performance of a year of penance will lead to marriages that are based on the fullest possible awareness of the facts of life.

THE EARLY FESTIVE COMEDIES: A MIDSUMMER NIGHT'S DREAM, THE MERCHANT OF VENICE

With *A Midsummer Night's Dream* (written about 1594–96) Shakespeare indisputably established himself as a great writer of romantic comedy. The confusions in *The Comedy of Errors* are amusing, and they are not totally devoid of implications concerning the complexities of life and man's blindness, but the implications are sporadic, and the play amuses rather than enraptures. *A Midsummer Night's Dream*, no less amusing, goes further and deeper by adding to the story of lovers' mistaken identities the actions of the royal classical lovers, Theseus and Hippolyta; the fairy lovers of folklore, Oberon and Titania; and the lovers in the craftsmen's play, Pyramus and Thisby. This rich collaboration makes *A Midsummer Night's Dream* an unexcelled comedy, a finely plotted and beautifully lyrical exploration of the nature of love, the nature of imagination ("fantasy"), the nature of reality or truth, almost, in short, the nature of life. (On the connections between the plots, see p. 61.)

Much of the play is derived from books: the story of Theseus and Hippolyta is taken from Chaucer's *The Knight's Tale*, perhaps reinforced with some details from Plutarch's *Lives*; Puck (or Robin Goodfellow) probably owes something to Reginald Scot's *Discovery of Witchcraft* as well as to old wives' tales that Shakespeare may have heard as a child in Stratford; Ovid's story of Pyramus and Thisby was studied in

Elizabethan grammar schools; and the ass-headed Bottom probably owes something to an Elizabethan translation of Lucius Apuleius' *The Golden Ass*. But the play does not smell of the lamp. Rather, it appears as effortless and as richly suggestive as a dream, and no less complex, beautiful, profound, or mysterious; and not least important, it is much more funny. Shakespeare might well have shared Nick Bottom's confidence: "I do not doubt but to hear them say it is a sweet comedy" (IV.ii.42–43). *A Midsummer Night's Dream* was probably written at about the same time as *Romeo and Juliet*. There are some resemblances between the two plays, most obviously in Lysander's speech ending with "quick bright things come to confusion" (I.i.141–49), which parallels abundant images in *Romeo and Juliet* of beauty quickly yielding to darkness (especially II.ii.119–20), and in the play-within-the-play concerning Pyramus and Thisby, who are in effect an ancient Romeo and Juliet. Aldous Huxley has complained that tragedy, in portraying only the single-minded, heroic strain in man, does not tell "the whole truth." No work of art tells the whole truth, of course, and it is unreasonable to judge a tragedy by such a standard. But one understands Huxley's comment: fine though *Romeo and Juliet* is, it seems a more mechanical, thinner, and less substantial exploration of life than *A Midsummer Night's Dream*.

Theseus feels that the lovers' story is "more strange than true," and at the end of the play Puck suggests that the audience can dismiss the entire play as a dream. But the dreams in the play are perceptions of reality: Hermia dreams (II.ii) that Lysander does not come to her aid while a serpent eats her heart, and when she awakens she finds that Lysander is gone, his love now fastened on another woman. Bottom dreams that he is an ass. Thus it may be an error to dismiss this dreamlike play and fail to see that the comedy is a profound treatment of love as a force, sometimes creative, sometimes destructive, sometimes wonderful, and sometimes laughable, but powerful and transfiguring.

In *The Merchant of Venice* (probably written in 1596) Shakespeare broadens his presentation of human personality.

Shylock and Portia, the opposed proponents of legalism and mercy, are much more fully realized characters than those in *A Midsummer Night's Dream*. But Bassanio, the male lover, is still not of very great interest. It is worth noting that Shakespeare's comic heroes are usually less witty and less resourceful, and therefore less interesting, than his heroines.

For many readers and spectators, Shylock is too interesting a character: the comic villain becomes a sympathetic and almost tragic figure, the wronged Jew towers above the petty Venetians. But such an interpretation is perhaps a misreading of the play, for it places too much weight on a few speeches in which the Venetians taunt Shylock and on other speeches in which Shylock quite rightly insists on his sufferings. The most famous instance of the latter is in III.i, when Shylock asks,

Hath not a Jew eyes? Hath not a Jew hands, organs, dimensions, senses, affections, passions?—fed with the same food, hurt with the same weapons, subject to the same diseases, healed by the same means, warmed and cooled by the same winter and summer as a Christian is? If you prick us, do we not bleed? If you tickle us, do we not laugh? If you poison us, do we not die? And if you wrong us, shall we not revenge?   (III.i.56–64)

One cannot easily dismiss this powerful speech by saying that it is only a justification for revenge, not a plea for tolerance. But to argue that Shylock's speech is what *The Merchant of Venice* is about is to turn away from much of the rest of the play; it is to overlook, for example, Portia's no less wonderful speech about mercy (IV.i.183–204), in which she points out that no one's deeds are so just that he does not require mercy. That Shylock cannot understand what Portia is talking about is an index of his severely limited nature. And so, with superb unconscious irony, Shylock says, "My deeds upon my head! I crave the law" (IV.i.205). Law is in fact what he gets, and only mercy saves him from the death penalty that the law imposes. What the play as a whole dramatizes is not the problem of a minority group suffering at the hands of a hostile society but the conflict of two ways of life, one concerned with hoarding (Shylock's "Fast bind, fast find,/A proverb never stale in thrifty mind"), the other with generous giving (Antonio's "My purse, my person, my extremest means/Lie all unlocked to your occasions," and Portia's "What is mine, to you and yours/ Is now converted"). Almost every element in the play is arranged to set forth some such fundamental opposition, but again the characters are not pale abstractions, and Shylock is no straw man. Shakespeare gives him powerful utterances and lets us see him fully, from the inside, as in the long speech quoted above. Probably no earlier character in Shakespeare so fully evokes from the hearer the response, "I understand exactly how that man feels." But the play is not about Shylock; rather, Shylock is an important character in a play about the triumph of generosity (love is a kind of giving), which transforms society into something more than a group of men who buy and sell and lend. The final scene is rich in intimations of a spiritually renewed society: "Let me give light," "riveted with faith unto your flesh," "my soul upon the forfeit," "you drop manna." In short, a new day is dawning ("it is almost morning")—which is not to say that sex and bawdry do not have their place, but only that this play about very human people is also a play with a great theme. Today, however, we inevitably regret that in conceiving one of his characters Shakespeare drew upon such anti-Semitic passages in the New Testament as Christ's reported words to the Jews: "Ye are of your father, the devil." We can, then, say that the play is anti-Semitic; but if we do, we will be missing the real point, and so we will do better to try to see what Shylock is and what he does, and to see him not as a Jew but as a certain kind of unloving, legalistic, death-dealing, diabolic man.

A BOURGEOIS COMEDY:
THE MERRY WIVES OF WINDSOR

The date of *The Merry Wives of Windsor* is uncertain, but a good case can be made for the spring of 1597. If that date is right, Shakespeare interrupted his work on the cycle of history plays concerning the reigns of Richard II, Henry IV, and

Henry V to write a comedy centering on Falstaff, who appears in an earlier play, *1 Henry IV*. According to legend, Shakespeare wrote the comedy in two weeks in response to Queen Elizabeth's desire to see Falstaff in love. The legend gains some support from the fact that the play is not in the romantic-comic vein that Shakespeare had been working in, perhaps because it was written quickly. It is Shakespeare's only comedy set in England, and it suggests the superiority of rural good sense over the arts of the courtier. In the play a character named Falstaff—who only sporadically has the wit of the Falstaff of *1 Henry IV*—attempts to seduce two married women and is ignominiously defeated. All the motifs of the play are found in earlier literature: a would-be seducer unknowingly reveals his plan to the lady's husband, escapes disguised as a woman, and is nearly suffocated or drowned. Possibly Shakespeare refurbished an old play, but if he did so, readers have not forgiven him for raising their expectations by calling one of the characters Falstaff and then failing to deliver the real Falstaff. As Dr. Johnson said, "Falstaff could not love, but by ceasing to be Falstaff." And although in this play Falstaff is sufficiently Falstaffian to be motivated by money, not love, still one senses a falling-off. The Falstaff of *Henry IV*, one feels, would have committed himself less totally to the plan and would, paradoxically, have made much more of it by his wit and imagination. In *2 Henry IV* Falstaff aptly says that he is not only witty in himself "but the cause that wit is in other men" (I.ii.9–10). In *The Merry Wives*, however, except in the first scene and in the beginning of the last scene, he has no worthy adversaries who bring out his own wit and whose wit he can sharpen. The witty Falstaff is not here because Prince Hal is not here; only the butt is here, and that is not enough. There is also a romantic plot involving a young man named Fenton, who is said to "speak holiday" and "smell April and May," but romance has only a small role in the play, which has strong affinities with Roman and Italian comedy: a braggart is humiliated, and a young man and a girl outwit the girl's parents and marry. Like *The Comedy of Errors* and

The Taming of the Shrew, The Merry Wives is fairly close to Roman comedy, and this means that it is highly farcical. Whatever the source, Shakespeare's handling of the plot is uncertain: for example, at the start Falstaff's old crew, Bardolph, Pistol, and Nym, appear; but after the first act they do nothing; the first scene introduces the idea of a quarrel between Falstaff and Justice Shallow, but nothing comes of it. Curiously this play, which seems so thin, is effective on the stage, and it is of special interest to those readers who see beneath the surface to the pattern of the ritual expulsion of Misrule or Riot, for Falstaff, an embodiment of Misrule, is dumped into the river and later is pinched and singed with candles by people disguised as fairies. The locale is contemporary Windsor, but there seem to be echoes of ancient rites of purification, such as survived in the Saint George plays (see p. 30). Still, the rituals in *The Merry Wives* remain jokes or tricks, cleverly engineered by the chaste wives, lacking the imaginative richness of the masquelike episodes in the other plays, which point to things "strange and admirable."

THE LATER FESTIVE COMEDIES: MUCH ADO ABOUT NOTHING, AS YOU LIKE IT, TWELFTH NIGHT

Near the turn of the century—just after he had finished his second tetralogy of history plays and was nearing the great tragedies—Shakespeare wrote three comedies that for many readers and spectators are the essence of Shakespearean romantic comedy: *Much Ado About Nothing* (1598–1600), *As You Like It* (1599–1600), and *Twelfth Night* (1600–02). These plays, like *The Merchant of Venice* and to a lesser degree *A Midsummer Night's Dream* and *The Two Gentlemen of Verona*, are plays of courtship. The assumption behind them is that despite momentary absurdities and pains, love liberates, enriches, and fulfills the lovers. But each play is unique, and it is perhaps best not to insist too loudly on their resemblances.

In fact, *Much Ado About Nothing* is not conspicuously romantic in any usual sense of the word. The main plot concerns the not very eloquent love of Claudio and Hero, the in-
terruption of that love (caused by the malicious Don John, a
descendant of the medieval Vice), and the restoration and completion of their love in marriage, when Hero is cleared from
slander and reunited with Claudio. To this pair of lovers
Shakespeare adds another, Beatrice and Benedick. They begin
as witty foes, are deceived into thinking that each is loved by
the other, and then, their pride conquered, they find that they
do indeed love each other. Thus in this parallel plot (it cannot
be called a subplot because it is no less important than the plot
of Claudio and Hero), lovers undergo a conversion, and the
somewhat self-righteous society of the early part of the play is
disabused of its illusions, thereby acquiring a new life. For
example, at the start Beatrice is characterized thus:

> But nature never framed a woman's heart
> Of prouder stuff than that of Beatrice.
> Disdain and Scorn ride sparkling in her eyes,
> Misprizing what they look on; and her wit
> Values itself so highly that to her
> All matter else seems weak. She cannot love,
> Nor take no shape nor project of affection,
> She is so self-endeared.   (III.i.49–56)

Both Beatrice and Benedick are liberated from this bondage
to the self, just as Claudio is liberated from his mistaken view
of Hero and from his subsequent grief for Hero's supposed
death. The prelude to this renewal is announced in verse, a
medium that the earlier parts of the play are not rich in:

> Good morrow, masters; put your torches out.
> The wolves have preyed, and look, the gentle day,
> Before the wheels of Phoebus, round about
> Dapples the drowsy east with spots of gray.   (V.iii.24–27)

Appropriately enough, the play ends with the marriage of
Claudio and Hero, the promise of a marriage between Benedick and Beatrice, and finally a dance giving visual representation to the transformed and now harmonious society.

Thoughts of the villainous Don John, now a prisoner, are not
allowed to intrude seriously upon the new-found joy: "Think
not on him till tomorrow. I'll devise thee brave punishments
for him. Strike up, pipers!" (V.iv.127–29). The play ends with
music and dancing: "All . . . sounds of woe," to quote from
a song in Act II, have been converted into "hey nonny, nonny."

Finally, a point should be made concerning Dogberry and
his fellows, the delightfully ignorant watchmen who through
a series of blunders apprehend the malefactors. The actions of
Dogberry and his fellows are one variant of the theme—recurrent in the comedies—that mistaken beliefs or errors have for-
tunate consequences. Benedick and Beatrice are deceived, and
the outcome is good; Claudio is deceived, and the outcome is
good (presumably his love for Hero at the end is greater because he has learned that his earlier mistrust was totally without foundation). Dogberry's errors too have a happy result;
moreover, his sublime self-confidence is a comic imitation of
the less amiable self-confidence of others in Messina. This is
not to say that we value him only because he plays an important role in the plot and because he contributes to the theme.
A richly comic figure, he affords us delight, and we would
value him for this even if he were irrelevant. In one of his
bumbling speeches he comes closest to stating the theme of
this comedy in which events happily conspire to give people
more than they deserve. The play shows us a world of people,
as Dogberry says, "condemned into everlasting redemption."

Like *A Midsummer Night's Dream* and *The Merchant of
Venice*, *As You Like It* presents two worlds. *A Midsummer
Night's Dream* moves from Athens, with its harsh law and its
harsh father, to the moonlit woods outside of Athens, where
lovers are transformed into their better selves; *The Merchant
of Venice* moves from the commercial world of Venice to the
moonlit world of Portia's Belmont. In *As You Like It* the
movement is from the court of the usurper, Duke Frederick,
to the Forest of Arden, where lovers find what they seek and
where the wicked are converted. Only Touchstone, the Clown,
and Jaques, the melancholy man, remain unimproved by Arden, a sort of hint of man's recalcitrance or self-conceit.

The play is full of "holiday foolery," but the foolery is not devoid of meaning, for it embodies an enduring vision of love and of the triumph of the gifts of nature over those of fortune. Various kinds of lovers are juxtaposed: the romantic young lovers, Rosalind and Orlando and Celia and the reformed Oliver; the prettified artificial pastoral figures, hard-hearted Phebe and her mooning Silvius, who thinks no man has ever loved as he loves; the low pastoral figures, old Corin, who has forgotten the ridiculous actions that love moved him to in his youth, and the young bumpkins William and Audrey; and finally the clown Touchstone, who remembers that when he was in love he kissed "the cow's dugs that her pretty chopt [chapped] hands had milked" (II.iv.47–48). Love is wonderfully displayed in the "strange capers" of these figures, and it is treasured even when it is mocked—as when Rosalind realistically warns Phebe against scorning Silvius' offers, saying, "Sell when you can, you are not for all markets" (III.v.60) or when Rosalind, concealing her love for Orlando, offers to cure him of the madness of loving Rosalind, and he replies, "I would not be cured" (III.ii.419). Nor, of course, would Rosalind or the audience want him cured. The love poems that Orlando writes are wretched (Touchstone drily offers to produce such rhymes "eight years together, dinners and suppers and sleeping hours excepted"), yet we would not have Orlando's rhymes improved; we value them for their delightful ineptitude. Rosalind herself is delightfully mocked, as in this bit of dialogue in which Celia (Aliena) prosaically reminds us that people in love can be very boring:

ROSALIND I'll tell thee, Aliena, I cannot be out of the sight of Orlando. I'll go find a shadow, and sigh till he come.

CELIA And I'll sleep.   (IV.i.213–16)

In short everything in the play, including the folly, is in Celia's words "O wonderful, wonderful, and most wonderful wonderful, and yet again wonderful." Not least wonderful are the improbable conversions of Oliver and the wicked Duke Frederick; again we are grateful for these improbabilities because we would not deny to anyone the possibility of finding joy by shedding self-centeredness. These two men come late to self-knowledge and its concomitant generosity of spirit, but better late than never. The play ends with "a wedlock hymn" and other strong hints of a transfigured world—though Jaques' refusal to join in the dance suggests that the new joyous order is less than total. The return of the exiles to the court is not a bit of cynicism discrediting their experience in the forest; rather, it brings the vitality and harmony of the forest into the court, which earlier in the play is a place of tyranny.

It is no derogation of *Twelfth Night* (probably written about 1600) to say that in it Shakespeare again uses several motifs from his earlier plays. Like *The Comedy of Errors* it involves twins—this time a brother and sister—who have been separated by a shipwreck and who are now (unknown to each other) in the same city. As in *The Two Gentlemen of Verona,* there is a girl disguised as a boy who serves the man she loves as a page, even to the extent of courting on his behalf a woman whom he woos. Like Benedick and Beatrice, who in *Much Ado About Nothing* are tricked into thinking that they love each other, Malvolio is tricked into thinking that Olivia loves him. Other similarities include a resourceful young woman (here Viola, in *The Merchant of Venice* Portia, in *As You Like It* Rosalind); deep affection between friends (here Antonio and Sebastian, in *The Merchant of Venice* Antonio and Bassanio); a fool (here Feste, in *As You Like It* Touchstone); and a somewhat Falstaffian character, Sir Toby Belch, who conveys an infectious delight in eating, drinking, and in using the purse of his betters. And in its festive spirit—for example, in its songs and mistaken identities—the play reminds us of episodes in *A Midsummer Night's Dream, The Merchant of Venice,* and *As You Like It.* (This spirit is what earns the play its name, for Twelfth Night is the Feast of the Epiphany, a holiday that England celebrated with antics involving a Lord of Misrule.) But despite similarities with some of the other plays, there are important differences. For example, though Viola resembles Rosalind in her cheerful courage and in her wit, because she lacks a confidante equivalent to Celia she conveys to us a delicate sense of melancholy absent from Rosalind.

Another difference between *Twelfth Night* and a predeces-
sor: in *The Comedy of Errors* the mistakes that cause bewil-
derment are largely physical—that is, they are literal cases of
mistaken identity caused by the presence of twins; but in
Twelfth Night there are more profound mistakes as well in the
failure of some of the characters to understand *themselves*.
Thus Malvolio not only misunderstands Olivia; he misunderstands his own nature and his role in society. Similarly, in pin-
ing for Olivia, Orsino does not see the egoism in his love, and
so, for example, the love song that he calls for (II.iv) is really
a song of self-love in which the lover calls attention to his
pathetic fidelity. At the end of the play Orsino is freed from the
torments of his own desires, which at the start pursue him "like
fell and cruel hounds." Olivia, too, grieving for her dead
brother, finds that she has mistaken the depth of her grief, and
she is liberated from her own "eye-offending brine." Thus despite the shipwreck and despite the trick played on Malvolio,
much of the trouble is not external but is rooted in self-deception. Against egoism and self-deception—neatly summed up
in Olivia's words to Malvolio, "O, you are sick of self-love"—is
a liberating generosity, not only in small details, as when
Antonio freely gives money to Sebastian (III.iii), but notably
in Viola, who gives herself to Orsino's effort to woo Olivia
even though Viola herself "would be his wife."

In *Twelfth Night*, then, although Shakespeare uses earlier
plots and characters, he is saying new things, especially about
the development of insight. One small index is provided by
the clown Feste, who, though by profession resembling Touchstone in *As You Like It,* is very different from Touchstone in
his wit and actions. Touchstone, however cynically, joins in the
procession to the altar, but Feste remains unwed, and after the
unregenerated Malvolio leaves and the lovers depart, Feste is
left alone on the stage to sing the Epilogue, with its melancholy
refrain, "For the rain it raineth every day." In *As You Like it,*
although the melancholy Jaques stands apart from the comic
resolution, he too looks forward to a new life, perhaps to be
gained through conversation with the regenerated Duke Frederick. But in *Twelfth Night* Feste—whose name suggests that

he is the very incarnation of festivity and whose role as professional entertainer may put us in mind of the playwright himself —stands apart, calling attention to the hardships of life. He does not thereby deflate the romantic vision, but he does complicate it; and with the advantage (or disadvantage?) of hindsight we may see an anticipation of the fool in *King Lear* and thus a suggestion—it is only a suggestion—of the affinities of *Twelfth Night* to the tragic world, where the fragility of order is explored.

THE DARK COMEDIES: ALL'S WELL THAT ENDS WELL, MEASURE FOR MEASURE

Two comedies, *All's Well That Ends Well* (1602–04?) and *Measure for Measure* (1604), are often called "dark comedies" or "problem plays." When the latter term is used, *Hamlet* (1600–01) and *Troilus and Cressida* (1601–02) are sometimes included as well. The term *problem play*, first used in the late nineteenth century to characterize some of Ibsen's work, denotes a play that examines a social problem rather than an unchanging fact of life, such as death. Thus it has been argued that *Measure for Measure* is about such problems as: Can a judge condemn a criminal for a crime that the judge himself is guilty of? May a person sin to save a life? But clearly *All's Well* and *Measure for Measure* are not primarily debates on such problems; if they are, they contain enormous amounts of irrelevant material. In another sense of the word, of course, the plays indeed are "problem" plays: critics do not know what to do with them.

The term *dark comedies*, then, is perhaps more useful: *All's Well* and *Measure for Measure* do not have the festive spirit that dominates *A Midsummer Night's Dream*, *The Merchant of Venice*, *Much Ado*, *As You Like It*, and *Twelfth Night*, and that is plentiful in some of the other comedies. Put most briefly, there is no green world and the lovers simply do not show as much delight as the lovers in the earlier comedies, where a spirit of playfulness abounds. *All's Well* has some close resemblances to the great romantic comedies—a resourceful heroine, disguise, coincidences, and finally a reunion between young people—but there is little of the joy of love in it. The play has the conventions but not the spirit of comedy. The nominal hero is not a young man in love; the closest he comes to being a suitor is when he resorts to bribery in an effort to seduce a woman.

The plots of both *All's Well* and *Measure for Measure* include actions that critics, especially those in the late nineteenth century, have found unpleasant. In both plays, for example, a man thinks he is seducing a woman but is tricked into sleeping with another woman whom he has rejected. The heroines in each play have struck some readers as unamiable, the nominal heroes as detestable. (And in *Troilus and Cressida* there is a faithless woman who by virtue of her faithlessness diminishes not only herself but her lover.)

In both plays there is clowning, but for some readers there is too much joking about syphilis, too much comic cowardice, too much disillusionment, and too much unpleasant behavior that reveals not merely folly but vice. *As You Like It* has a usurping duke and a wicked elder brother, but we see little of them and they reform; during most of the play we are diverted by the lovers in the Forest of Arden. *Twelfth Night* has a shipwreck and the unregenerated Malvolio, but the shipwreck takes place off stage with no real harm done, and Malvolio is funny rather than criminally vicious. Of the earlier comedies, perhaps *Much Ado* comes closest to—though it is still far away from—*All's Well* and *Measure for Measure*. In *Much Ado* Don John is villainous, the hero Claudio is churlish, the witty lovers Benedick and Beatrice are on the whole satiric rather than romantic, and the setting is never varied by an excursion into a green world. But in *Much Ado* there is the sublimely bumbling Constable Dogberry, who by his ineptitude saves the situation. As one of the villains says to the wiser folk in *Much Ado*, "What your wisdoms could not discover, these shallow fools have brought to light" (V.i.230–31). In the two dark comedies, however, evil is fended off only by vigorous effort. In *As You Like It* the characters do little more than disport themselves in the woods until the two wicked characters repent, and in *Twelfth Night* Viola relies on time to solve the problem: "O time, thou must untangle this, not I;/It is too hard a knot for me t' untie" (II.ii.40–41). But in *All's Well* the heroine (like a good counselor in a morality play) must vigorously—almost desperately—pursue her wayward husband, saving him from fornication by a trick in which she interposes her own body, and in *Measure for Measure* the good duke must keep bustling—somewhat to his discredit—if the lecherous Angelo is not to have his way. Time, of course, has a role in these plays too, but in both plays the central characters must energetically make use of it, rather than, as in *Twelfth Night*, await it. We will find something of this sense of strain in the last comedies too, the so-called romances, especially in *The Tempest*.

That the plays have less festivity or playfulness, and that they have potent sources of evil, is indisputable. On the other hand, if we are repelled by what is delicately called the "bed trick," and if we resent the fact that the caddish Bertram is "dismissed to happiness," perhaps we are deficient in a sense of playfulness. That these comedies are not festive comedies is perhaps no more significant than that they are not tragedies or histories: they are what they are, and though we may feel that they are not fully successful, we can be thankful for them. Nor should we characterize the plays as cynical: *All's Well* especially has honorable characters who not only utter noble sentiments but act virtuously and effectively; *Measure for Measure*, although short on characters who fully engage our affections, is ultimately based on the generous view that evil intentions, if unacted and repented of, do not deserve punishment, and the play concludes with contrition and forgiveness.

Finally, a point about the origin of these dark comedies should be made: readers have tended to date them near to *Hamlet* and *Troilus* and near to each other (though *All's Well* often has the abundant rhyme of the earlier plays) and have assumed that around 1600 Shakespeare became pessimistic, perhaps because a mistress was unfaithful or because Essex' revolt was abortive. Perhaps; and it is true that many of his subsequent plays show a deep sense of the complex admixture of good and evil. But, despite our tendency to believe that works of art are deeply personal, Shakespeare's plays may not reflect his mental ups and downs; rather, some elements in the dark comedies may represent his response to a literary fad, perhaps stimulated by Ben Jonson, whose satiric comedies regularly scourge folly: in *All's Well* Bertram and Parolles are revealed as fools; in *Measure for Measure* the ascetic Angelo betrays his ideals and is exposed. (*Troilus and Cressida* too is a thoroughly ironic play: the heroine is false, her noble lover is gulled, and Thersites and Pandarus are at least as gross as the world they comment on.) If Shakespeare was indeed responding to Jonsonian satiric comedy, his response was characteristically Shakespearean, for even the dark comedies finally are charitable: no one is everlastingly cast out, Bertram and Angelo (like Mankind in a morality play) are redeemed, and if there are not the joyous feasts that conclude some of the earlier comedies, there is nevertheless, as the braggart Parolles in *All's Well* says, "place and means for every man alive." Parolles, in fact, is at last welcomed to Lafew's table, although Lafew was the first to see through his deceptions: "Though you are a fool and a knave," Lafew tells Parolles, "you shall eat."

THE ROMANCES:
PERICLES, CYMBELINE, THE WINTER'S TALE,
THE TEMPEST, THE TWO NOBLE KINSMEN

If the conjectured dates of the dark comedies are right (about 1602–04), during the next few years Shakespeare wrote only tragedies: *King Lear* (1605–06), *Macbeth* (1605–06), *Antony and Cleopatra* (1606–07), *Timon of Athens* (1604–09), and *Coriolanus* (1607–09). But he ended his career with a return to comedy, that is, with plays that end happily: *Pericles* (1608–09), *Cymbeline* (1609–10), *The Winter's Tale* (1610–11), and *The Tempest* (1611). To these can be added two plays on which he may have collaborated with John Fletcher, *Henry*

VIII (1612–13) and *The Two Noble Kinsmen* (1613). *Henry VIII,* an historical play, is discussed with the histories, but in a broad sense it is "comic," like Dante's *Divine Comedy,* for it moves from trouble to joy, ending with the christening of the infant Elizabeth I and the promise of a joyous future.

Shakespeare's last plays are in various ways fairly closely related, and critics usually call *Pericles, Cymbeline, The Winter's Tale,* and *The Tempest* "the romances." Except for *The Tempest,* like nondramatic romances the plays are concerned with wonderful actions that cover a long period. The title page of *Pericles* calls attention to this aspect of the play: "the true relation of the whole history, adventures, and fortunes of the said prince, as also the no less strange and worthy accidents in the birth and life of his daughter Marina." A dominant motif in these four plays is the restoration of losses: Pericles regains his wife Thaisa, who had been thought dead, and his daughter Marina, who had been abducted by pirates; King Cymbeline regains his two sons, abducted in infancy; in *The Winter's Tale* friends who had quarreled are after many years reunited, and the king regains his lost daughter; in *The Tempest* an exiled duke regains his dukedom, and the King of Naples regains his son. Of course, the earlier comedies too have such restorations: in *The Comedy of Errors* a long-separated family is at last reunited; in *As You Like It* a duke regains his dukedom. But *The Comedy of Errors* is mostly about comic errors in identity, and *As You Like It* is mostly above love. In contrast, the last plays in large measure are about restoration; moreover, the restoration of losses is closely related to a sense of renewal consequent upon suffering and repentance. In some degree they seem to be a development from the dark comedies, which emphasized man's fallen condition and yet concluded with forgiveness, and from the tragedies. It is almost as though *King Lear* were given a happy ending, with Lear and Cordelia reunited. In the romances the stuff of tragedy—exile, jealousy, even death—usually takes place early (in *The Tempest* the exile of Prospero takes place before the play begins), and the plays focus on the post-tragic regeneration and reunion. In *The Winter's Tale* the first three acts are ominous, including mad and destructive jealousy, a storm, death, and the exposure of an infant to the elements, but then the scene changes to springtime and a pastoral world, and the last two acts work toward a resolution. One cannot conceive of a happy ending added to the first three acts of *King Lear* (the pre-Shakespearean play *King Leir* did restore Leir to his throne, but Leir had not gone mad on the heath). As Charles Lamb said of such a possibility, in his essay "On the Tragedies of Shakespeare":

A happy ending—as if the living martyrdoms that Lear had gone through—the flaying of his feelings alive, did not make a fair dismissal from the stage of life the only decorous thing for him. If he is to live and be happy after, if he could sustain this world's burden after, why all this pudder and preparation—why torment us with all this unnecessary sympathy? As if the childish pleasure of getting his gilt robes and scepter again could tempt him to act over again his misused station—as if at his years, and with his experience, anything was left but to die.

This is finely said; and yet the romances are concerned with a stage of life that puts great suffering into a new perspective. Pericles says to the gods, as Lear could not, "Your present kindness/Makes my past miseries sports" (V.iii.39–40).

Although there are deaths in *Pericles, Cymbeline, The Winter's Tale,* and *The Two Noble Kinsmen,* the plays have a serenity that separates them from the festivity of the early comedies, the stress of the dark comedies, and the agony of the tragedies. Consider the idealized and somewhat etherealized heroines in the last plays: Marina in *Pericles,* who miraculously remains unspotted though she is sold into a brothel; Imogen in *Cymbeline;* Perdita in *The Winter's Tale;* Miranda in *The Tempest,* who has seen no men other than her father and a bestial servant; and Emilia in *The Two Noble Kinsmen.* For the most part the heroines of the earlier comedies are witty and resourceful, but the later heroines, notable for their innocence, have a sort of Snow White quality. (Viola, in *Twelfth Night,* if we compare her with the more energetic Rosalind of *As You Like It,* or with her counterpart in the source, suggests that even before he wrote the romances, Shakespeare was movıng toward a heroine less conspicuously active and more an object of reverence.)

Coupled with this emphasis on innocence and the restoration of losses is a strong sense of providence, made explicit by visible manifestations of the deity: Diana appears in *Pericles* and Jupiter appears in *Cymbeline,* Apollo's oracle is quoted in *The Winter's Tale,* and Duke Prospero has magical powers in *The Tempest.* In *The Two Noble Kinsmen* prayers are made before the altars of Mars, Venus, and Diana, and the deities respond. In these plays, to quote from *Pericles,* we strongly feel that we see "virtue preserved from fell destruction's blast,/ Led on by heaven and crowned at last."

The note of innocence and the sense of providence are strengthened by the pastoral settings of some of these plays and by the images of the sea and storms, which contrast with the pastoral settings. Shakespeare used a shipwreck as early as *The Comedy of Errors,* but in the last plays the sea and the storms are under the control of providence. In *Pericles* the lovely Marina is born during a storm at sea, and when she is finally reunited with her father a "great sea of joys" rushes upon him (V.i.196); in *The Tempest,* Ferdinand says, "Though the seas threaten, they are merciful" (V.i.178). The emphasis on innocence and providence makes the plays hover at the edge of allegory. The characters seem a bit flatter or thinner, and if we prefer the earlier more complex characters we may find in the last plays too much freedom or casualness not only in the characterization but in the plotting and the versification. The commonest reply to this is that Shakespeare deliberately used thin characters, improbable situations, unidiomatic speech, and relatively free versification in order to move to the transcendent post-tragic vision behind the happenings. Having written festive comedies, darker comedies that treat romantic love somewhat skeptically, and tragedies, Shakespeare ended his career with a sort of play that has elements of all the earlier types but contains a new vision. Other explanations have been offered: Shakespeare was bored with the theater and was now interested only in making experiments in poetry itself; or Shakespeare, especially after the ac-

quisition of the indoor theater at Blackfriars in 1608, was trying to attract a more courtly audience, one that preferred spectacular, allegorical masques and plays remote from common
life; or Shakespeare was responding to James I's vision of himself as a peacemaker; or for some unknown reason at the end
of his career Shakespeare was returning to the loose romantic
dramas of his youth; or Shakespeare was losing his grip. In any
case, these plays are related, but it is time to look at them
singly.

The earliest of the romances, *Pericles,* is of uncertain date
and even uncertain authorship; it was not included in the
First Folio, perhaps because the compilers of the Folio believed it to be written in large part by a hand other than
Shakespeare's. In any case, most critics hesitate to attribute the
first two acts to Shakespeare, chiefly because the poetry in
these acts is very weak. (It is hard to tell exactly how weak, because the text is badly corrupted in places.) The plot is derived
from a narrative that Shakespeare used as early as *The Comedy of Errors,* when he attached to Plautus' *Menaechmi* the
old tale of a family dispersed by a storm at sea and reunited
after much wandering. In *Pericles* a king is reunited with his
wife and daughter after abundant grief, and the story deals
with "this great miracle," a pattern that must in part be derived from the medieval miracle plays dramatizing a saint's life.
There are storms in *Pericles* as in *King Lear,* but in *Pericles*
the storms are ultimately seen to be providential. Thaisa,
thought dead, is coffined and dropped into the sea, but she is
miraculously restored to Pericles; his daughter, abducted and
sold to a brothel, remains a virgin and converts her potential
customers; Pericles, almost dead from sorrow, is miraculously
restored to life by his long-lost daughter. If we wished to find
an emblem for the play's theme, we would perhaps find it in
the device on the hero's shield, "a withered branch that's only
green at top" (II.ii.42). The world seems a barren, deathly,
tempestuous place, but for the innocent and the patient there
is, at the top, the possibility of new life.

The editors of the First Folio put *Cymbeline* among the
tragedies, perhaps because they felt that a play in part con-

cerned with a Roman invasion of Britain could not with pro-
priety be put among the comedies; nor could it be put among
the histories, since it includes romance material and deals with
a legendary pre-Christian Britain, whereas all the history plays
deal with medieval or early Renaissance England.

Like *Pericles, Cymbeline* is concerned with exile and restoration: the two princes, abducted from court and brought
up in simple surroundings, at last are restored to the king,
thus bringing back to the court the virtues of a healthy, simpler experience. And the maligned princess, who had fled the
court and who is thought dead, is reunited with her husband
(also thought dead), who now fully perceives her virtue. Like
Pericles too it is set in a pagan world, but with markedly
Christian overtones. For example, when Jupiter says, "Whom
best I love I cross; to make my gift,/The more delayed, delighted" (V.iv.71–72), it is not merely the word *cross* (here a
verb, meaning "to thwart") that evokes a Christian framework
but the whole idea that the heavenly powers chasten those
whom they love (compare the Bible's "Whom the Lord loveth,
He chasteneth"). Suffering is transcended, and all losses are
restored: "The fingers of the pow'rs above do tune/The harmony of this peace" (V.v.466–67). But viewers and readers
have found that the harmony is achieved only after a bewilder-
ing diffusion of interest, and one cannot easily dismiss Dr.
Johnson's reference to "the folly of the fiction, the absurdity of
the conduct, the confusion of the names and manners of different times, and the impossibility of the events in any system
of life." The dialogue is often obscure; characterization in general counts for less than striking theatrical situations, and because there is no central character the focus is in doubt. The
play mingles three motifs: pastoral matter of princes brought
up close to nature, political-historical matter of Rome's conquest of Britain, and a story of love, which includes a disguised princess who apparently dies and comes back to life. In
some degree, the play is Shakespeare's fusion of the histories
(there is something about England's role in the world, and
peace with Rome is achieved), the tragedies (exile, war, and
death), and the comedies (courtship and marriage).

Like *Pericles, The Winter's Tale* is derived from a prose narrative that includes much of the stuff of the Hellenistic romances: an exotic pagan setting, an abandoned infant, an oracle, a storm, a long separation, love, and ultimately a reunion between those separated. In some matters Shakespeare lessens the operations of chance; for example, in the source the young lovers by the accident of shipwreck find themselves in Sicily, where the girl is reunited with her father, but in *The Winter's Tale* they deliberately set out for Sicily. But the play as a whole has an air of the wonderful or, as in King Leontes' sudden fit of jealousy (I.ii), of the unpredictable and the irrational. Against this are elements that on a casual view can be called realistic—notably the roguish peddler Autolycus and the sheep-shearing festival in Act IV, where comedy and English character-types and customs appear in remote Bohemia. More precisely, however, this pastoral "realism" is not realism at all but another variety of romance; it is the romance no longer of the exotic but of the simple or "natural," for Perdita at the shepherds' festival gives us a picture of the vitality of innocence, in a setting of fertile nature. But the play as a whole presents a very different world from that of *As You Like It,* with its delightful Forest of Arden. The seriousness of the issues is insisted on: Leontes' jealousy at the start causes the death of his little son and of others, and it initiates sixteen years of separation from his wife and his daughter. The first three acts, in short, are a winter's tale, tragic in tone. But in III.ii, when the infant Perdita is abandoned on a stormy coast and found by shepherds, there is a turn: "Now bless thyself," one shepherd says to another, "thou met'st with things dying, I with things newborn." Act IV begins with Time, who tells us that sixteen years have passed, and soon Autolycus appears and introduces a note of spring in a song about daffodils. Ultimately, Perdita is restored to her repentant father Leontes; her mother Hermione—thought dead not only by Leontes but by the audience—is also restored, the most astounding presentation of the motif of reconciliation in the play. The restoration to Hermione of the lost Perdita, who is associated with the spring, is a sort of analogue to the Greek myth of the seasons, in which Proserpina is rescued from the lower world and restored to her mother Ceres in the spring. It resembles, too, the Christian pattern of redemption. At the reunion—the resurrection, we might almost say—Hermione's first words are a prayer to the gods to pour their graces upon her daughter's head, and there is the implication here, as in *The Tempest,* that the innocent love of the children redeems the errors and sins of their fathers. Like *Pericles,* the play ends happily with expressions of joy, but it cannot be grouped with the festive comedies, not only because its first half has the violence of tragedy but also because its ending is suffused with deeper solemnity. If we must classify the play, we might take a hint from Polonius and call it tragical-comical-pastoral.

Like some of the early comedies, which are ultimately indebted in varying degrees to late Greek and Roman comedy, *The Tempest* has a shipwreck (compare *The Comedy of Errors* and *Twelfth Night*), an irritable father (compare Egeus in *A Midsummer Night's Dream*), and a character who more or less manipulates the plot (compare Rosalind in *As You Like It*). Like *The Comedy of Errors,* possibly Shakespeare's earliest comedy, it obeys the ancient traditions of unity of time and place: the play spans only a few hours and occurs in one locale. But despite these and other resemblances, the unusual amount of spectacle in *The Tempest*—and, more important, the serious tone—ties the play to Shakespeare's other last plays. The old conventions are here, but with new meanings: *The Tempest* is concerned with guilt and forgiveness, royal children, wonderful quasi-resurrections, and finally reunions. "These are not natural events, they strengthen/From strange, to stranger" (V.i.227-28). The pastoral setting, implying the freshness and vitality of nature, prominent in parts of *Cymbeline* under the thin disguise of the Welsh countryside and in *The Winter's Tale* in the Bohemian shepherds' feast, is presented in *The Tempest* in the mysterious island—though this island means different things to different people: to one observer the grass looks "lush and lusty," but to another the grass is "indeed tawny." Pastoralism appears too in the masque of Ceres and Juno and the dance of nymphs and harvesters.

Again there is a shipwreck, and again the results prove benef-icent. Those who are cast upon the island find, strangely, that their "garments, being, as they were, drenched in the sea, hold, notwithstanding, their freshness and glosses, being rather new-dyed than stained with salt water" (II.i.64–67). This note of renewal or regeneration is variously sounded throughout the play. Suffering brings renewal: "Some kinds of baseness/ Are nobly undergone, and most poor matters/Point to rich ends" (III.i.2–4). Even Caliban, more a beast than a man, though acknowledged by Prospero as Prospero's educational failure, at last resolves to "seek for grace," thus suggesting that the most rudimentary kind of human being can make some moral progress. Not Caliban but Antonio, Prospero's brother, is the real failure, for Antonio's silence in the recon-ciliation scene suggests the limits of Prospero's power: the shipwreck manufactured by Prospero can only provide the opportunity for repentance, but it cannot force repentance, for a man has the freedom to remain recalcitrant if he wishes. Still, much goodness has been found:

> In one voyage
> Did Claribel her husband find at Tunis,
> And Ferdinand her brother found a wife
> Where he himself was lost; Prospero his dukedom
> In a poor isle; and all of us ourselves
> When no man was his own.   (V.i.208–13)

The sense of providence, strong in the last plays, is embodied in *The Tempest* chiefly by the magician Prospero, who raises and allays the storm that helps to regenerate and reconcile. (But Prospero, though in some ways godlike, is not God; be-fore the play began he was so enraptured by "secret studies" that he shirked the cares of the state, and during the play he learns to pity and, apparently, to forego vengeance and to for-give—somewhat grudgingly—the wrongdoer.)

Because *The Tempest* is probably the last play that is entirely Shakespeare's (he seems to have had a collaborator for *Henry VIII* and *The Two Noble Kinsmen*), there is a tendency to see in Prospero, the magician who can call up visions but who at the end breaks his staff and abjures his "potent art," a picture of Shakespeare putting down his pen and contemplating retirement to Stratford. There is no great harm in such a reading as long as it does not reduce the play to an autobiographical scrap. It would be a pity to see in *The Tempest* only a farewell to the theater and to fail to notice that Prospero goes not to retirement but to the active role of ruling in Milan as the duke. The meaning of this play, like the meanings of Shakespeare's other plays, finally is complex. But this is not to say that the play is obscure or cryptic, although the Baconians find a cryptogram in the two lines at the end:

> As you from crimes would pardoned be,
> Let your indulgence set me free.

What was Shakespeare *really* saying at the end of his last play? The Baconian answer is that the letters in these lines can be rearranged into this message: "Tempest of Francis Bacon, Lord Verulam; do ye ne'er divulge me, ye words." Such, for some, is Shakespeare's final message; no matter that this message has three *a*'s in it and Prospero's lines only two.

There remains a postscript. *The Two Noble Kinsmen* was first published in 1634 (though apparently written in 1613), and the title page ascribes it to John Fletcher and William Shakespeare. Readers have often disagreed with the ascription, but there is no uniformity in their disagreement; some attribute the entire play to Fletcher, some to Shakespeare. The ascription of the title page seems more reasonable than either of these extreme positions. Like the other late romances *The Two Noble Kinsmen* is rich in spectacle, which is perhaps related to the fact that Shakespeare's company was at the time using the Blackfriars theater, playing to audiences with courtly tastes. The play opens with a nuptial procession (described in some detail in the first stage direction) before the Temple of Hymen, and it contains processions to the altars of Mars, Venus, and Diana, as well as a country dance. Like *Pericles, Cymbeline,* and *The Winter's Tale, The Two Noble Kinsmen* is based on what Ben Jonson called a "mouldy tale"—in this case, the old narrative romance that Chaucer's Knight tells in *The Canterbury Tales*. And like Shakespeare's other late plays, and unlike many of his earlier plays, characterization is flatter, resulting sometimes in sharp contrasts. It is occasionally so thin in this play that the effect is of characterlessness. Unlike the romances that are unquestionably Shakespeare's, however, *The Two Noble Kinsmen* is not concerned with the regeneration of men who have sinned or erred or with the restoration of old losses, although at the end of the fifth act there are passages that strongly remind us of the other last plays:

> O cousin,
> That we should things desire which do cost us
> The loss of our desire! That nought could buy
> Dear love but loss of dear love!   (V.iv.108–11)

But the bulk of the dramatic action does not greatly support this sort of thing, and the play's ending, in which Arcite wins Emilia but at the cost of his life, differs markedly from the reconciliation that characterizes the endings of the other romances. Much of *The Two Noble Kinsmen* is more mannered, more prettified, and more ceremonious but also more hollow than the romances. It has a pathos, a politeness, and a pointlessness that we associate with Fletcher. Possibly it is best to see *The Two Noble Kinsmen* as largely Fletcher's, with Shakespeare—not always at top form—writing perhaps Acts I and V and adding passages here and there.

8

The English History Plays

Evidence suggests that there were about two hundred Elizabethan history plays, most of them written within a fairly short period, between 1588 or so and 1600. Before the defeat of the Spanish Armada in 1588 there seems not to have been a single play on English history written for the public stage, though there were dramas on biblical, classical, and legendary heroes and villains, popular entertainments dramatizing Saint George of England and Robin Hood, and, for a limited audience, some academic dramas on English history with a very heavy infusion of political morality, notably *Gorboduc* (1561). For about a decade after the defeat of the Armada, the English history play—a genre apparently invented by Shakespeare or developed by him out of the most meager dramatic precedents—was in vogue in the public theater. Of the eighteen plays that Shakespeare wrote up to the end of 1599 nine were on English history. But he then abandoned the genre, returning to it only once, at the end of his career, about 1613.

If we include plays on classical history (*Julius Caesar, Antony and Cleopatra,* and *Coriolanus*) and on legendary British history (*King Lear, Macbeth, Cymbeline*), almost half of Shakespeare's plays can be called historical, but the editors of the First Folio, in separating the histories from the comedies and tragedies, classified as history only those ten plays that dealt with relatively recent British history. These plays they arranged chronologically by date of subject matter (not of composition), beginning with *King John* and ending with *Henry VIII*. Three of these plays had been published earlier in individual volumes as tragedies: *3 Henry VI* as *The True Tragedy of Richard, Duke of York*; *Richard III* as *The Tragedy of King Richard III*; and *Richard II* as *The Tragedy of King Richard the Second*. Conversely, *King Lear*, included in the Folio among the tragedies, was first published as *The True Chronicle History of the Life and Death of King Lear*, and *The Merchant of Venice*, a comedy, was first published as *The Most Excellent History of the Merchant of Venice*. The history play evidently was not (and is not) a clearly defined genre; but it is still useful to consider the ten history plays of the Folio as a group. The subject matter—political events in England—relates these plays to one another in a way that the Roman plays, for example, are not related, though it is not quite true to say that the sole concern of the plays is politics and that the real protagonist is England (people keep breaking in). Even those plays that have a tragic shape, *Richard II* and *Richard III*, stand apart from such tragedies as *King Lear* and *Macbeth* by their primary emphasis on several characters engaged in political actions. Although political actions do occur in the tragedies, the primary emphasis in the tragedies is on what might be called the private matters of a central figure—for example, Lear's relations with his daughters and movement toward self-knowledge and Macbeth's relations with his conscience.

The first four plays—three on Henry VI and one on Richard III—cover a continuous period from 1422 to 1485 and so may be considered a tetralogy; four later plays—*Richard II, 1 Henry IV, 2 Henry IV*, and *Henry V*—cover an earlier continuous period from 1398 to 1422 and so may be considered a second tetralogy. The two tetralogies thus run from 1398 to 1485, when Henry VII, the first Tudor monarch and the grandfather of Queen Elizabeth, ascended the throne. This was a period of civil war between the houses of Lancaster and York. Henry Bolingbroke, of the house of Lancaster, banished by Richard II in 1398, in 1399 returned and soon pushed Richard II from the throne, becoming Henry IV. But the Yorkist family pressed its claim to the throne and not until the defeat of Richard III of York, by Henry, Earl of Richmond, who became Henry VII, was the struggle settled. (Henry VII, the first Tudor monarch, was descended from Owen Tudor of Wales, who had married Henry V's widow, Catherine.) These plays were presented singly, not as tetralogies, but insofar as each play looks both backward and forward and tells only a piece of a larger story, the tetralogies bear some resemblance to the great medieval cycles of miracle plays, which spanned time from the Creation to the Day of Judgment and which also allegedly presented history, showing such events as Herod's Slaughter of the Innocents and the subsequent punishment visited upon him. For example, in the first play of Shakespeare's second tetralogy, *Richard II,* Bolingbroke takes the throne from Richard, the next two plays reveal the suffering and turmoil consequent upon this act of usurpation and the working out of evil, and the last of the four plays, *Henry V,* reveals the restoration of peace and unity in England under a monarch said to be "the mirror of all Christian kings." Like the medieval cycles, Renaissance history plays were presumably not only entertaining but also instructive, for Elizabethans assumed that one learns from history how to behave. History, properly understood, was morality, as an Elizabethan schoolboy found when he read his Caesar and Sallust and Livy, for he saw that rebellion is inevitably punished. In the dedication to *A Mirror for Magistrates* (1559), a collection of narrative poems on the fall of rulers, the editor addresses "the nobility and all other in office" and informs them that "here, as in a looking glass, you shall see (if any vice be in you) how the like hath been punished in other heretofore, whereby admonished, I trust it will be a good occasion to move you to the sooner amendment." (Another aspect of this influential book is discussed in connection with Shakespeare's tragedies, pp. 139–44.) History also eloquently recorded the heroic deeds of great men, thus persuading the reader to virtuous action. In 1592 Thomas Nashe defended the stage against puritanical attacks, by seizing on the moral implications of history plays. First, he held, they revive "our forefathers' valiant acts," serving as a "reproof to these degenerate effeminate days of ours"; second, "in plays, all cozen-

age, all cunning drifts over-gilded with outward holiness, all
stratagems of war, all the cankerworms that breed on the rust
of peace, are most lively anatomized: they show the ill success
of treason, the fall of hasty climbers, the wretched end of
usurpers, the misery of civil dissension, and how just God is
evermore in punishing of murder."

This emphasis on history as morality serves also to link
the history play to certain late morality plays that had concerned themselves with politics. Sometimes Shakespeare's
plays strongly remind us of the abstractions of the old moralities, as when in *2 Henry VI* a character says,

> Ah, gracious lord, these days are dangerous:
> Virtue is choked with foul ambition,
> And charity chased hence by rancor's hand;
> Foul subornation is predominant,
> And equity exiled your highness' land.   (III.i.142–46)

The political moralities, in turn, helped to give rise to a
type that can be called the moral history. For example, John
Bale's *King John* (1539, revised between 1558 and 1563) is
indebted to the morality play for such characters as Nobility,
Civil Order, Sedition, and Dissimulation, but it approaches
the history play when Sedition becomes Stephen Langton,
Private Wealth becomes Pandulphus, Usurper Power becomes
the Pope, and so on. Moreover, King John is not deceived by
evil counselors, as he would be in a morality play; rather, he
is an ideal Christian and the defender of the widow England,
though he is finally poisoned by Dissimulation, who has become the monk Simon of Swinstead. In some sense, then, Bale's
King John is concerned not with the trial of a soul but with an
historical failure. Only after John's death is England rescued
from the wicked. In this respect Bale's play is closer to the
miracle play than to the morality play; indeed, the Interpreter
in the play compares John to Moses, who sought to withstand
"proud Pharaoh for his poor Israel."

The Tudor history play, then, is not a period piece evoking
the atmosphere of a particular age; rather, though it dramatizes the past, it is supposed to be timeless, for the sins and

the political machinations of one age are very like those of another, and man, so the theory held, should learn from the past how to behave in the present. Contemporary problems of government are seen not through allegory but through episodes from the past. This idea is still with us, in such expressions as "History repeats itself" and "Those who cannot remember the past are condemned to repeat it." For the Elizabethans, parallels between reigns and between rulers readily suggested themselves. Queen Elizabeth, when reading some documents concerning Richard II (who had been deposed) is said to have angrily exclaimed, "I am Richard II." And in 1601 Essex arranged for a performance of Shakespeare's *Richard II* the day before his rebellion against Elizabeth, presumably to show the populace that a monarch might be deposed. This sense of the intimate connection between past and present, by the way, perhaps diminishes pedantic criticism of such anachronisms as the infamous clock in *Julius Caesar* or the hats in the same play. To draw Rome as rather like Elizabethan London was a way of affirming the essential sameness of human existence from century to century.

But though Shakespeare's history plays show the painful consequences of usurpation and tyranny, they are not sermons; a central character, representative of mankind, no longer dominates the plays, and they are filled with personalities who color or overshadow the political lessons. If the plays sometimes seem to illustrate a text in the first book of homilies, *An Exhortation Concerning Good Order and Obedience to Rulers and Magistrates* (1547)—"Take away kings . . . and such estates of God's order . . . no man shall sleep in his own house or bed unkilled; . . . there must needs follow all mischief"—they do so not simply from a desire to urge subjects to be dutiful but from an understanding of the ways people act and react. To take a simple example: with the aid of Worcester and others Bolingbroke deposes Richard II; in the next play, *1 Henry IV*, Bolingbroke (now Henry IV) finds that he cannot trust his former allies, and Worcester finds that he cannot trust the new king, for he knows that Henry will always suspect him of feeling that he has not been sufficiently rewarded; moreover, Henry will always suspect Worcester of contemplating yet a second overthrow of a king. If there is a moral here, it is not obtrusive; the play is chiefly about people, rather than about providence's government of the realm, though it is true that as in medieval drama there is a sense of retribution: crimes are punished.

That the plays are not overtly didactic is perhaps the more remarkable in view of their relation to the moral histories and their immediate derivation for the most part from Raphael Holinshed's *Chronicles of England, Scotland, and Ireland* (1577; second edition, used by Shakespeare, 1587). About 1501 Henry VII, the first Tudor, brought Polydore Virgil from Italy to rewrite English history from the Tudor point of view, and Virgil's work, along with that of several successors (notably Edward Hall), was more or less incorporated into Holinshed's enormous history book. (Strictly speaking, Holinshed's own work also became incorporated into the book bearing his name because the second edition was not really his; it was produced by collaborators after his death.) As part of this rewriting of history, Richard III, for example, who was pushed from the throne by Henry VII, was made into a monster, first by Sir Thomas More and Polydore Virgil, then by Hall, who borrowed from them, and then by Holinshed, who used their material. Henry VII, of course, was idealized. Holinshed borrowed not only many of the details of his predecessors but also the overall view that the history of England showed the workings of God: Henry IV's usurpation of the throne led to a century of war, but God watched over England, punished the wicked, and at last placed the Tudors on the throne. Occasionally this note is heard in Shakespeare's history plays, especially in the last history, *Henry VIII*, which celebrates the birth of Queen Elizabeth and which suggests that England is again Eden. But for the most part the plays give us a picture of men forging their own destinies, though of course such a picture is not incompatible with the idea that God works in mysterious ways, leaving man's will free but finally seeing that His will is done.

THE FIRST TETRALOGY:
1, 2, AND 3 HENRY VI, RICHARD III

The three plays on Henry VI, covering about fifty years from the death of Henry V (1422) to the murder of Henry VI (1471), are troublesome, and some critics claim that much in these plays was written by a hand other than Shakespeare's. (If the plays are entirely by Shakespeare, it may well be that he originated the English history play, for it is not certain that any plays of this type preceded them on the public stage, the moral histories being closer to the morality plays than to these chronicle plays.) Probably the most widely accepted view today is that the three plays are chiefly Shakespeare's, written between 1588 and 1592, and that *1 Henry VI* was written after *2 and 3 Henry VI;* possibly *1 Henry VI* is Shakespeare's revision of an older play. Of the three, *1 Henry VI* is notably the most episodic; it more or less chronicles a period, but it does not always pull the events into a unity (though of course it can be said that the play is united by depicting the conflict of good and evil or by its theme of the weakness of England under a vacillating king). There is some attempt to appeal to patriotism—the "brave" Talbot is an English paragon who has captured fifty French fortresses—and some attempt to warn Englishmen against disunity—Talbot is "entrapped" by "the fraud of England, not the force of France" (IV.iv.36–37). On the whole, the play is a series of scenes, some of which are effective, especially in establishing antitheses (as between the heroic Talbot and the wicked Joan and between honest Humphrey Duke of Gloucester and the corrupt Bishop of Winchester), but some of which lead nowhere, chiefly, it seems, because Shakespeare did not yet have that insight into human nature that he was to achieve in his later historical plays. After all, as Henry James said in *The American Scene,* history "is never, in any rich sense, the immediate crudity of 'what happens,' but the much finer complexity of what we read into it and think of in connection with it." Yet something too must be forgiven a dramatist who sets out to dramatize material whose shapelessness Holinshed (Shakespeare's source) desperately explained in this manner: "Thus often-times varied the chance of doubtful war."

That Shakespeare saw in the history play something other than a mere exhortation of patriotism, or a mere illustration of providence's concern for England, is revealed also in *2 and 3 Henry VI*. In *2 Henry VI* the king evokes pity but little respect; Richard Plantagenet, Duke of York, evokes horror; and Cade and his low followers evoke unsympathetic laughter —though such is Shakespeare's generosity that even Cade at his death evokes some pathos. Only Duke Humphrey is much of a credit to England, and he is murdered halfway through the play. Like *1 Henry VI*, *2 Henry VI* contains scenes that do not lead to further action and that at first glance perhaps seem extraneous—such as Duke Humphrey's exposure of Sim-cox, who claims to have been miraculously cured of blindness (II.i), and the death of Thomas the armorer at the hands of his apprentice (II.iii). But in fact these scenes are thematically relevant to the whole: the first of these episodes helps to demonstrate the good sense that Humphrey has and that the king lacks; the second helps to demonstrate the disorder that pervades the realm, showing on a low level the chaos that exists also among the nobility. The material concerning Jack Cade's rebellion provides York with the excuse that he must bring back his army from Ireland to put down the lowly Cade,. and in Cade's ignorance and cruelty there is yet another image of the horrors of civil strife engendered by the nobles. More-over, with hindsight, looking on this play from, say, the vantage point of *Julius Caesar,* where the tragedy divides into two parts, the first centering on the conspiracy against Caesar and the second on the civil war, we can see that in *2 Henry VI* Shakespeare gave some unity to the first half of the play by focusing (more or less) on the murder of Duke Humphrey and then concerning himself in the second half with civil war.

The brutality that is present throughout the play in sharply realistic scenes (compared with the more allegorical *1 Henry VI*) is neatly illustrated in a single sentence when Cade re-plies to Lord Say's self-defense: "He shall die, an it be but for pleading so well for his life" (V.vii.107–08). That brutality engenders further brutality is well dramatized throughout the play but perhaps nowhere more effectively than in V.ii, when young Clifford finds that his father has been slain by York:

> York not our old men spares;
> No more will I their babes: tears virginal
> Shall be to me even as the dew to fire,
> And beauty, that the tyrant oft reclaims,
> Shall to my flaming wrath be oil and flax.
> Henceforth I will not have to do with pity:
> Meet I an infant of the house of York,
> Into as many gobbets will I cut it
> As wild Medea young Absyrtus did.   (V.ii.51–59)

The mythological reference in the last line—a simile occupying exactly one end-stopped line—is a bit of gratuitously and obtrusively displayed learning, but on the whole the speech is a fine one, especially in the powerful simplicity of "Henceforth I will not have to do with pity."

3 Henry VI continues the dramatization of chaos from about 1455 to 1471. In the first act young Clifford fulfills the promise he made in *2 Henry VI* not to spare "babes" when he kills York's youngest son, the Earl of Rutland. Other deaths follow in this highly episodic play, but the episodes are thematically united in their emphasis on the breadth of the destruction, as in the scene balancing a son who has killed his father against a father who has killed his son and in the death of the young Prince Edward, which is a variation on the death of young Rutland. *3 Henry VI* ends with Richard murdering Henry VI, and with the accession of Edward IV; but despite Edward's concluding line—"For here, I hope, begins our lasting joy"— the ending is not an ending, because (as Edward's feeble "I hope" almost implies) bloodshed is to continue in *Richard III*. Richard's distinctive blend of irony and cruelty is already present in the first scene of *3 Henry VI*, when instead of recounting his exploits in battle, as his brothers do, he throws down the severed head of the Duke of Somerset and says, "Speak thou for me, and tell them what I did" (I.i.16). Richard continues this tone to the end of the play, when he holds up his bloody sword and says, "See how my sword weeps for the poor king's death" (V.vi.63). Between these speeches he vows "to catch the English crown . . ./Or hew [his] way out with a bloody ax" (III.ii.179–81). Richard's subsequent bloody deeds are the substance of the fourth play of the tetralogy, *Richard III*.

The Tudor chroniclers had reported Richard's enormities, and Shakespeare followed them in describing a man capable of every inhumanity. In the three plays in which Richard appears, he is compared to (in alphabetical order) a bear, a boar, a dog, a hedgehog, a lizard, a spider, a tiger, a toad, and a wolf, as well as to three mythical beasts, a basilisk, a cockatrice, and a hellhound. But why is he capable of every sort of villainy? And why is he not simply repellent to us? The answer to the first question briefly is that Richard (like Aaron in *Titus Andronicus* and Iago in *Othello*) is descended from the medieval Vice, the diabolic trickster who delighted in villainy. The answer to the second question is probably that Richard's energy and enthusiasm in his villainy offer esthetic pleasure; he continually sees himself as an actor performing the most outrageous roles, and though we deplore his atrocities we delight in his verve. We can attribute Richard's own delight in activity and power to the fact that as a hunchback he cannot know the normal satisfactions that come from respect and love, and in a long speech in *3 Henry VI* (III.ii.146–71) Richard suggests that since he is barred from normal delights he will dedicate himself to the conquest of "such as are of better person than myself." But Shakespeare sees Richard too as the unmotivated Vice; indeed, Richard sees himself as the Vice: "Thus, like the formal Vice, Iniquity,/I moralize [interpret] two meanings in one word" (III.i.82–83). (The Vice regularly deceived people by double meanings.) This aside to the audience, inviting an appreciation of Richard's theatrical skill as well as of his theatrical origin, helps us to see him as an expert performer rather than as a moral monster. (In an aside at the very end of *3 Henry VI* he invites the audience to see him as no less skilled in deception than Judas.) Thus Richard is sometimes the passionate man, defrauded by the ac-

cident of his misshapen body; but at other times (and most
often) he is a spirit of deceit, given to witty asides and soliloquies, entertaining in his very mischief, and inviting the audience to delight in his resourcefulness even though his energy is
misdirected:

> I do the wrong, and first begin to brawl.
> The secret mischiefs that I set abroach
> I lay unto the grievous charge of others.
>
> .   .   .
>
> But then I sigh, and with a piece of Scripture
> Tell them that God bids us do good for evil;
> And thus I clothe my naked villainy
> With odd old ends stol'n forth of holy writ,
> And seem a saint when most I play the devil.
>
> (I.iii.323–25, 333–37)

The most notable of Richard's successes, the winning of Lady
Anne (whose husband and father he had killed), is accom-
plished, as he says, with no aid other than "the plain devil
and dissembling looks." We deplore his immorality but we
admire his sense of theater. The play is, in the usual sense of
the word, highly "theatrical," a tissue of contrivances that
not only undo the unsuspecting and the overconfident (Hast-
ings, for example, gloats at the destruction of his enemies even
as we know he will soon be destroyed) but also undo the con-
trivers. And these repetitions of incident, often ironic or anti-
thetical, have a parallel of sorts in the language, where repetitions (sometimes of entire lines, sometimes of words, sometimes
of initial consonants) and antitheses are abundant; they can
be glimpsed even in the soliloquy just quoted, where "*s*ecret
*m*ischiefs" are "*s*et abroach," and where Richard explains
that he seems a saint though he plays the devil.

Action and rhetoric combine in yet another way: historically
Margaret played no part in the events, for she had gone to
France and died there, but Shakespeare seems to use her as a
Senecan Fury, a creature who moves others to vengeance and
whose rather formal curses embody destiny, specifically in the
shape of retributive justice. The idea of retribution, however,
is found not only in Seneca but also in some miracle plays,

where such tyrants as Pharaoh and Herod come to a bad end, and also in much of *A Mirror for Magistrates.*

Unlike Pharaoh and Herod, however, Richard is a villain-hero, not a mere villain. By the time he says (V.viii.201–02) "There is no creature loves me;/And if I die, no soul will pity me" and "I myself/Find in myself no pity to myself," he has won from the audience some degree of pity. He had aimed at achieving esteem, but he finds at the end he has no self-esteem. To this degree at least he joins the company of tragic heroes whose attempt to achieve some good (as they conceive it) proves to have an ironic outcome and gives us a sense of greatness undone. In short, *Richard III* draws the gist of its plot from the *Chronicles,* but it draws its understanding of the plot and its methods from earlier drama. Superimposed on these theatrical traditions is the Tudor chronicler's view that God expressed His will in English history: England was providentially united by the victory of the rather colorless Richmond, who, by defeating Richard III, "one that hath ever been God's enemy" became Henry VII, the first Tudor monarch. The marriage of Richmond (Lancastrian) to Princess Elizabeth (Yorkist) united the factions of England and thus ended the Wars of the Roses.

KING JOHN

There is a good deal of uncertainty about the date of *King John* (conjectures range from 1590 to 1597) and some uncertainty about that of *Richard II* (conjectures range from 1595 to 1597). Whichever play was earlier, it is clear that having written an historical tetralogy Shakespeare decided to continue writing history plays but not to carry the story beyond where he had left it, with the accession of Henry VII in 1485. To have carried it forward would have brought him up to the sixteenth century—dangerously close to his own times. Instead he went backward, to King John (1167?–1216) and to Richard II (1367–1400). But parallels with contemporary politics were not thereby excluded: King John's rejection of the Papal Legate's authority (III.i) was often seen as an anticipation of Henry VIII's break with the Roman Catholic Church and of Elizabeth's position after the pope excommunicated her in 1569; the deposition of Richard II, as Shakespeare's company found out, was for a while taken as a comment to the effect that Elizabeth might appropriately be deposed.

King John was a figure of considerable interest to the Elizabethans, but not because he signed the Magna Carta, which Shakespeare does not even mention. Because he defied papal authority medieval chroniclers saw in John a wicked king; for the same reason, most Tudor chroniclers saw in John a Protestant martyr. When about 1538 the militant Protestant John Bale wrote an anti-Catholic political morality play, he sought to avoid anything reminiscent of the old religious drama and so went to English history and chose King John as his central figure. But unlike Bale's play, Shakespeare's *King John* is not vehemently anti-Catholic, despite the king's rebuff to the Papal Legate; nor is the play calculated to appeal throughout to an Englishman's patriotism, for John is a usurper and he is responsible for the death of his nephew Arthur, the legitimate heir. In fact, Shakespeare's King John is a mixture of the two historical traditions; he owes something to the Catholic tradition of the lawless king and something to the Protestant tradition of the nationalistic martyr. This blend of traditions is pretty far from *Richard III*, where good and evil are clearly separated; and it is also pretty far from any simple view of English history. In *King John* the historical material is used as the stuff of moral decisions, and with hindsight we can see John as an anticipation of Shakespeare's Brutus, a man whose political motives are honorable (John seeks to strengthen England) but who becomes involved in moral guilt (complicity in Arthur's death). And so John degenerates after III.ii (though he is unaccountably called "our great King John" in V.iv) and dies unheroically, while Faulconbridge, the engaging satiric commentator, rises. Faulconbridge's final speech is a patriotic address:

> This England never did, nor never shall,
> Lie at the proud foot of a conqueror
> But when it first did help to wound itself   (V.vii.112–14)

Perhaps more interesting than this dubious assertion is the fact
that Faulconbridge is a serious yet at times comic character
who wittily and shrewdly comments on the passing scene.
None of the earlier histories has so complex a figure; indeed,
it is partly the characterization of Faulconbridge that makes
the date of 1590 seem too early for this play. But Shakespeare
is full of surprises.

THE SECOND TETRALOGY:
RICHARD II, 1 AND 2 HENRY IV, HENRY V

Richard II (1595), the first play of Shakespeare's second tetralogy, is very different from *King John,* partly because it is given
a tragic shape. Its antecedents include those narrative poems
in *A Mirror for Magistrates* and its predecessors that set forth
the fall of kings, and Richard sees himself as a fit subject for
such a story:

> For God's sake let us sit upon the ground
> And tell sad stories of the death of kings:
> How some have been deposed, some slain in war,
> Some haunted by the ghosts they have deposed,
> Some poisoned by their wives, some sleeping killed,
> All murdered—for within the hollow crown
> That rounds the mortal temples of a king
> Keeps Death his court, and there the antic sits,
> Scoffing his state and grinning at his pomp,
> Allowing him a breath, a little scene,
> To monarchize, be feared, and kill with looks,
> Infusing him with self and vain conceit,
> As if this flesh which walls about our life
> Were brass impregnable; and, humored thus,
> Comes at the last, and with a little pin
> Bores thorough his castle wall, and farewell king!   (III.ii.155–70)

Later in the play he urges his queen to "tell . . . the lamentable tale of me,/And send the hearers weeping to their beds" (V.i.44).

With Richard's fall comes Bolingbroke's rise, giving us the first extant English play in which two characters are pitted against each other. (In Marlowe's *Edward II* the weakling protagonist, who must have influenced Shakespeare's conception of Richard, is opposed not by an individual but by a group.) Viewed one way, as the Duke of York explains to Richard (II.i.195–99), the play is the tragedy of an irresponsible king who makes the mistake of confiscating John of Gaunt's estate, thus bringing Gaunt's son Bolingbroke back to England to claim his inheritance and finally to depose and indirectly murder Richard. Viewed another way, the play is a political play exploring the nature of kingship, the duties of subjects, and the realities of political struggles. Twentieth-century critics have tended to stress the second view, but for the general reader—who is not likely to be familiar with Tudor historical writing or to have in mind the three subsequent histories (*1 Henry IV, 2 Henry IV,* and *Henry V*) that deal with the results of the deposition—the play probably remains a tragedy; we remember not the political machinations (these somehow seem to be a rather formal background) but the wretched fallen king, who anticipates Hamlet in his neurotic sensibility, his changeableness, and his grief—which is not to say that there are not enormous differences between Richard and Hamlet.

If *Richard II* is a tragedy, or even if it is a political play, what sort of king is Richard? Critics divide into the softhearted and the hardheaded. The first group sees Richard as a poet, a delicate and tender prince too fine for this gross world (according to W. B. Yeats, he belongs to that group of people who lack a commonplace "rough energy" but have something more precious, such as "contemplative virtue, . . . lyrical phantasy, . . . sweetness of temper"). The hardheaded group turns this view inside out and says that if Richard is a poet, he is a very bad poet, a man in love with words but indifferent to people other than himself, and ignorant of himself because he swathes his actions in such abundant metaphors that he loses sight of the actions themselves. This second view is now dominant, and much stress has been put on Richard's tendency to use highly figurative language. It should be mentioned, however, that Richard is not the only one in this play to use elaborate figures. The truth is that the play is highly figurative throughout; even the Gardener speaks metaphoric verse; and Bolingbroke, widely regarded as businesslike, describes his own exile thus:

> Must I not serve a long apprenticehood
> To foreign passages, and in the end,
> Having my freedom, boast of nothing else
> But that I was a journeyman to grief?   (I.iii.270–73)

Bolingbroke's figure of an exile as an apprentice, heightened by his pun on *"journey*man," should caution us against speaking too easily of Richard as a man whose fault is that he plays on words, or whose strength is a sensitivity to language. Probably the truth is that Shakespeare had only recently—perhaps because he had been writing two narrative poems and dozens of sonnets—developed as a poet and was now writing not merely drama in somewhat mechanical verse but drama in highly lyrical poetry. Like *Romeo and Juliet* and *A Midsummer Night's Dream, Richard II* is among Shakespeare's first plays to employ iterative imagery—that is, recurring images that help to give unity to the play. The exact dates of these three plays are uncertain (probably all were written between 1594 and 1596); *Richard II* may indeed be Shakespeare's first play to use such imagery. There are many images, for example, comparing England to a garden. These are most obvious in III.iv, when the Gardener and his man compare *their* commonwealth, the garden itself, to Richard's garden, England. The man asks his master why they should

>   in the compass of a pale,
> Keep law and form and due proportion,
> Showing, as in a model, our firm estate,
> When our sea-wallèd garden, the whole land,
> Is full of weeds, her fairest flowers choked up.   (III.iv.40–44)

The Gardener replies, now varying the figure by seeing Richard himself as a plant:

> He that hath suffered this disordered spring
> Hath now himself met with the fall of leaf:
> The weeds which his broad spreading leaves did shelter,
> That seemed in eating him to hold him up,
> Are plucked up root and all by Bolingbroke—
> I mean the Earl of Wiltshire, Bushy, Green.   (III.iv.48–53)

And so on. But such imagery is not confined to this scene, where it is almost inevitable. John of Gaunt earlier compares England to the Garden of Eden (II.i.42), and goes on to say that Richard has degraded it to a wretched farm; Bolingbroke characterizes Bushy and others as "the caterpillars of the commonwealth,/Which I have sworn to weed and pluck away" (II.iii.165–66); Richard later is said to be a rightful king "planted many years," and if Bolingbroke usurps the crown "the blood of England shall manure the ground" (IV.i. 127,137); in his final speech Bolingbroke regrets that "blood should sprinkle me to make me grow" (V.vi.46).

Although there are manifest dangers in reading a play as though it were a short lyric poem (the spectator, after all, cannot hold each image in his mind and then relate it to the next occurrence of the image), it is clear that *Richard II* lends itself to this sort of reading. It should be noted too that some of the imagery is reinforced by the action. There are, for example, images and gestures of rising and falling (the play shows Bolingbroke's rise and Richard's fall), as in Richard's invitation to "sit upon the ground/And tell sad stories of the death of kings" and in Richard's address to Bolingbroke, who is kneeling before him: "Up, cousin, up, your heart is up, I know" (III.iii.142). In short, actions as well as images have their effect. If in *Richard II* Shakespeare was writing a *poetic* play, he was also writing a poetic *play*.

In the two plays on the reign of Henry IV and the play on the reign of Henry V Shakespeare abandoned the tragic structure that he had used to give shape to *Richard II* and returned to a looser, chronicle arrangement. He returned also to the abundant use of prose and of comedy, both of which are absent from *Richard II.* These plays, however, do not merely plod through the happenings of the reigns as Shakespeare encountered them in history books, though the titles of the plays sometimes lead a reader to think they are shapeless. *1 Henry IV* (1597), for instance, was first published under this title page (which includes the earliest extant use of the word *history* as a theatrical designation): *The History of Henry the Fourth; with the battle at Shrewsbury between the King and Lord Henry Percy, surnamed Henry Hotspur of the north. With the humourous conceits of Sir John Falstaff.* But the play is not merely a history or chronicle with a big battle and some "humorous conceits"; rather, it is largely organized by showing Henry IV visited by retribution, by juxtapositions of related characters, and by the story of the reformation of Prince Hal. (More precisely, the play is organized around the apparent reformation of Hal, since Hal even in his rakish days is never really sullied and therefore does not need to reform, though he does need to put off pleasure and to accept duty.) Another way of looking at the structure is to say that the play is organized around the conflict of Henry IV and Worcester, and this conflict is resolved on the battlefield in V.iv when Henry's son Hal defeats Worcester's nephew Hotspur. If one must come up with a single unifying formula, perhaps it will do to say that the play is about the revelation of Hal's political virtue. *1 Henry IV,* then, bears some resemblance to the morality plays on the motif of the Prodigal Son. To put it perhaps too simply, Hal is a figure of Mankind, tempted toward a riotous life by Falstaff; but he recognizes his duty and returns to help his father conquer the rebellious lords. A bit more precisely, Hal allows Falstaff to entertain him with images of riotous behavior but does his duty when required. The nature of honor is wonderfully explored, sometimes in explicit speeches about honor, as in Hotspur's rather huffing lines about plucking "bright honor from the palefaced moon" (I.iii.192–206) and in Falstaff's pragmatic catechism to the effect that honor is a mere "word, . . . air" (V.i.127–41) and again in his later comments on the "grinning honor" that the

dead Sir Walter Blount has won (V.iii.32–33, 58–63). Sometimes the nature of honor is explored in actions, as when Hal
defeats Hotspur and (by way of contrast) when Falstaff shams
death. And of course the explicit discussions fuse with the actions: for example, a moment after Falstaff concludes that
honor is only a word, Worcester dishonorably fails to tell
Hotspur of "the liberal and kind offer of the king" (V.ii.2).
While exploring honor, specifically in the political world,
Shakespeare also explores the nature of kingship, partly by
arranging his scenes so that they illuminate his themes. In the
beginning of the play the king is weak and shaken, but he looks
forward to a time of security when he can make a crusade to
Jerusalem. News soon comes to the effect that a rebellion
(recall that Henry himself had been a rebel against Richard
II) prevents this journey. This first scene alludes to Northumberland's son Hotspur, and the king, commenting on his own
scapegrace son, expresses his envy of Northumberland, who
has "so blest a son." The next scene shows the scapegrace with
Falstaff, and in the course of the scene it becomes clear that
Hal is not quite what his father thinks. The third scene, showing the king dealing with his potentially rebellious allies,
brings Hotspur on the stage, and the disloyalty of the young
man who a bit earlier had been praised by the king is now
explicit. Such juxtapositions are the work of a dramatist, not
a chronicler. Lest there be any doubt, it is worth mentioning
(to take only the most obvious example) that Shakespeare made
Hotspur—who in fact was thirty-nine at the Battle of Shrewsbury—much younger, pairing him off with Hal, who in fact
was sixteen at Shrewsbury.

The play, then, is carefully constructed. However, it seems
likely that at the start Shakespeare did not know just where
he was going. Judging from the early part of the play, with its
talk of rejecting Falstaff, it rather looks as though Shakespeare
planned to end the play with the death of Henry IV, the
coronation of Hal, and the rejection of Falstaff; but midway
through the play he perhaps found that too much material
remained to be fitted into the little space remaining, and so
he ended with the victory at Shrewsbury and saved the addi-

tional material for another play, *2 Henry IV*, which he probably wrote shortly after.

A spectator watching *2 Henry IV* (1597–98) must start with the assumption that Hal is still unreformed and unreconciled with the king, although reformation and reconciliation take place in *1 Henry IV*. That is, this sequel again shows Hal shirking filial duties and then removes Hal from the tavern and reconciles him with the king. But despite this resemblance in plot, the plays are very different, for *2 Henry IV* is a darker play, and if its theme can be summed up in a word, that word is not honor or valor but justice. But it is not only that the theme is different; the world of the play is different. In *2 Henry IV* there are numerous images of diseases: Northumberland is sick (or crafty-sick); the king is sick and during the play dies; the kingdom is sick ("You perceive the body of our kingdom/How foul it is, what rank diseases grow"), and perhaps most important for our present purpose, Falstaff is sick. When we first meet him he is inquiring about the doctor's opinion of his urine (I.ii); later he says, "I am old, I am old" (II.iv.277), and the Chief Justice describes him as "blasted with antiquity" (I.ii.186). Moreover, in *2 Henry IV* Falstaff—now fretful rather than joyful—is associated with darker companions, the doddering and corrupt Justice Shallow, the craven braggart Pistol, and the whore Doll Tearsheet, the last two of whom have beaten a man to death. There is humor in the play, but on the whole the humor is of a different sort, tinged with darkness. In *1 Henry IV* there are delightful bouts in which Hal and Falstaff heap abundant entertaining abuse on each other, but in *2 Henry IV* Hal and Falstaff have only two scenes together: in the first of these scenes (II.iv) there is some of the old fooling, but the scene ends with Hal's brusque "Give me my sword and cloak. Falstaff, good night"; in the second scene (V.v.47 ff.) Hal rejects Falstaff, in a famous speech beginning "I know thee not, old man." The speech is justly famous, but for some critics it is notorious because Hal (in their view) callously turns off an old companion, revealing that accession to the throne has narrowed his sympathies to those of only another politic man who knows how to get ahead in the world.

Against this view it can be argued that at his coronation Hal
exhibits the public virtue that Richard lacked; he can scarcely
embrace the man who represents disorder, and in this play—as
opposed to *1 Henry IV*, where he is more genial—Falstaff embodies not an engaging comprehensiveness but disorder or
anarchy. At least at a crucial moment, when he learns that Hal
has become king, he utters a joyous yet dangerous bullying cry:

> Let us take any man's horses; the laws of England are at my com-
> mandment. Blessed are they that have been my friends, and woe to
> my Lord Chief Justice!   (V.iii.140–43)

Falstaff's moment of joy is undercut even more by the fact
that the audience, having already seen Hal take the Lord Chief
Justice as his new guide, knows that Falstaff must be rejected.
In a sense, the end of the play brings us back to the beginning,
when in the Prologue Rumor talks about "smooth comforts
false" that help to destroy men. (Another aspect of this motif is
the deceptive words by which Prince John destroys the rebels;
in *1 Henry IV* heroism plays a part in putting down rebellion,
but not in *2 Henry IV*.) However we take the rejection of Falstaff, whether as an indication of Hal's increase in political
virtue or of his decrease in private virtue (even if we grant the
political necessity of the rejection, are we not disturbed by
Hal's apparent lack of regret?), *2 Henry IV* remains a very different play from *1 Henry IV*. But to say that *2 Henry IV* is the
darker of the two is not to say that it is black; despite the emphasis on sickness, corruption, and death, there is some mirth
and some nobility, not least when the wretched Feeble, a conscripted recruit, says, "I will do my good will, sir. You can have
no more" and, with a pun on *debt/death*, "A man can die but
once. We owe God a death. I'll ne'er bear a base mind. And't
be my destiny, so. And't be not, so. No man's too good to
serve's prince" (III.ii.239–42).

Possibly before Shakespeare wrote *Henry V* (1598–99) he
wrote *The Merry Wives of Windsor*, a comedy with Falstaff,
but that play does not concern us here; for despite Falstaff's
presence, *The Merry Wives* makes no use of historical ma-
terials. In *Henry V* Shakespeare finished the tetralogy that he

began with *Richard II* and then developed in two plays on the
reign of Henry IV. In *Henry V*, he returned to the rather episodic technique of his earliest history plays, in which the chief
principle of arrangement is chronology, though of course he
was highly selective in what he presented. (Perhaps he was not
sufficiently selective in the comic material that more or less
alternates with the historical material. It is all funny enough,
but some of it seems stuck in. Still, one is grateful for all that
one gets, and Mistress Quickly's description of the death of
Falstaff, in II.iii, is the sort of unnecessary but superb thing
that a less comprehensive dramatist might have deprived us
of.) The play is usually regarded as a dramatic epic, a kind of
narrative of the heroic doings of "the mirror of all Christian
kings," a king who, because he is not weak like Richard or
tainted like the usurper Henry IV, can lead his country to
glory in a just war against France. This interpretation may be
right, but it is too simple for some readers, especially readers
living in an age when war is inglorious. As a result, a counter-
interpretation has developed: the war is shown to have its
seamy side (the church supports it in order to avoid a tax,
some of the soldiers are disreputable, and the cruelty is apparent), and Henry is less an ideal king than an adept politician,
a man of narrow sensibilities (had he not narrowed himself
when he rejected Falstaff, saying he "despised" the life that
Falstaff stood for?), at ease uttering hypocrisies and playing
upon men. Yeats, whose praise of Richard II was quoted earlier, put it thus: "Having made the vessel of porcelain Richard
II, Shakespeare had to make the vessel of clay Henry V. He
makes him the reverse of all that Richard was. He has the gross
vices, the coarse nerves, of one who is to rule among violent
people." Thus Henry's lament on the treachery of Scroop,
Cambridge, and Grey (II.ii.127–42), which moves him to say
"I will weep for thee;/For this revolt of thine, methinks, is
like/Another fall of man," has led critics to comment sourly
that Henry had betrayed Falstaff and goes on to betray his
other early friends. One sympathizes with critics who find complexity here, and one cannot brush off the complexity simply
by saying that it exists only in the minds of the critics, for as

Robert Frost once remarked, a poet is entitled to the credit for everything that a reader finds in his work. Still, the three traitors themselves confess their treachery; nowhere is there an explicit statement that lends support to the idea that we are not to take Henry's words at face value. Similarly, though it can be said that the cowardly Pistol is a parody of Hal, deflating Hal's heroic speeches, it can be replied that Hal is Hal and that Pistol does not refute him but rather sets him off more clearly. And yet these replies do not finally convince; the impression remains that despite Henry's public virtues, the private man has something unattractive about him. He is a hero, enormously competent and often engaging, but we somehow feel he is a bit too self-satisfied, armed with a tendency to fend off the moral problems of war by using casuistry, and (in his last speech in IV.i) by bargaining with God.

Despite this ambiguity in *Henry V,* the play remains simpler than the two parts of *Henry IV.* Yet it does not lack variety: *Henry V* is not written in a single idiom, say that of "Once more unto the breach, dear friends, once more;/Or close the wall up with our English dead." There is also admirable prose, some of it in dialect, some of it bawdy, some of it so deceptively near to common speech that we must remind ourselves that its "naturalness" is no less artful than the more conspicuous "big" speeches. For example, on the eve of the Battle of Agincourt a common soldier describes Henry's show of courage thus:

He may show what outward courage he will; but I believe, as cold a night as 'tis, he could wish himself in Thames up to the neck; and so I would he were, and I by him, at all adventures, so we were quit here. (IV.i.113–17)

Possibly we can accept *Henry V* a bit more easily if we think of it as the happy final act in a four-act play (*Richard II, 1 Henry IV, 2 Henry IV, Henry V*) on the history of England from 1398 to 1415, working its way through weakness, deceit, and violence to as harmonious a conclusion as would be appropriate, "Congreeing in a full and natural close,/Like music." In fact, like a comedy the play ends with a betrothal. But the end of a comedy is assumed to be permanent, with the implication that the lovers live happily ever after. Shakespeare saw history as an unending series of ups and downs, and so at the very end of the play the Chorus reminds us that although Henry won a bride and France, "the world's best garden," Eden was again lost during the reign of Henry VI.

THE LAST HISTORY: HENRY VIII

At the end of his career, probably around 1613, Shakespeare returned to English historical drama, which he had put aside about 1599 with the completion of *Henry V*. Possibly he felt in 1599 that he could come no closer to the present than he had already come, for in *Richard III* he had reached the Tudor period; probably he felt he wanted to try to work in a different form. He turned to Roman history, writing the tragedy of *Julius Caesar,* and then to a variety of comic and tragic subjects. But about the time of his retirement from the theater he returned to English history for some reason, and wrote (perhaps in collaboration with John Fletcher) another play drawn largely from his old sourcebook, Holinshed's *Chronicles. Henry VIII* is a curious play; it is not at all like Shakespeare's earlier histories, which (although varied) combine penetrating analyses of monarchy with a sense of England engaged in military conflict, working out from one reign to the next the sins and errors of previous years. But the Prologue to *Henry VIII* announces that we will not get the usual battle scenes, and we do not. *Henry VIII* relates the falls of three eminent people, Buckingham, Katherine, and Wolsey, and the near-fall of Cranmer, sometimes accompanied by declamations and interspersed with elaborate pageants.

To the extent that *Henry VIII* has more visual splendor than Shakespeare's earlier histories it has affinities with *Cymbeline, The Winter's Tale,* and *The Tempest*—that is, with the other plays Shakespeare wrote at the end of his career. This affinity is strengthened by the presence in *Henry VIII* of some of the themes found in the other last plays, notably the themes of patience in adversity and the innocence and vitality of a new generation. But for some readers and spectators, in *Henry VIII* these themes do not succeed in uniting the splendid episodes, which are not tightly connected by causal relationships. *Henry VIII* looks back to *A Mirror for Magistrates* in its account of the falls of illustrious people (the predominantly good Buckingham, the totally innocent Katherine, and the ambitious and scheming Wolsey), and it concludes with a burst of religiously tinged patriotism celebrating the birth and christening of the infant Elizabeth, who will introduce a new golden age. The three falls taken together involve the stuff of tragedy—innocence and guilt, intrigue, and bad luck; but these motifs are separated in the play and the effect is that of oversimplification, except insofar as we can pull the episodes together by seeing in the play a providential hand governing England. For example, in the punishment of Wolsey we can see, with a little effort, the king as dispenser of divine justice. Perhaps, too, there is a contrary ironic view, for although the play ends with Cranmer, Cromwell, and Anne Bullen high on Fortune's wheel and with the prophecy of greatness for England under Elizabeth and her successor, Shakespeare's audience knew that the first three had in turn been brought low, and it may have felt that Elizabethan glory started to fade even as Elizabeth did.

For three centuries stage history has proved that *Henry VIII* is effective in the theater, though never more so than at what probably was its premiere in 1613 when (quite literally) it brought the house down: cannon shot off in accordance with a stage direction (I.iv.49) ignited the thatched roof, and the Globe Theatre burned to the ground. England's greatest age of drama was over.

9

The Tragedies

A Renaissance dictionary defines tragedy as "a lofty kind of Poetry and representing personages of great state and matter of much trouble, a great broil or stir: it beginneth prosperously, it endeth unfortunately or doubtfully, contrary to a comedy." (A comedy "beginneth sorrowfully, and endeth merrily, contrary to a tragedy.") Broadly speaking, Shakespeare's tragedies follow this pattern, except for *Hamlet,* where the hero is not "prosperous" at the beginning. For instance, at the start of the play Othello is newly married to Desdemona; Lear is almost a demigod giving away kingdoms; Macbeth has conquered on the battlefield and been elevated in rank. Moreover, all of Shakespeare's tragic heroes, with the possible exception of Romeo and Juliet, are "personages of great state," but even Romeo and Juliet are the children of important families. (The assumption was that nobleness involved an inherent superiority derived from high birth; persons worthy of their rank radiated this.) And each of these tragic heroes "endeth unfortunately."

The idea that tragedy involves a fall from a height was commonplace in the Middle Ages, though at that time "tragedy" denoted a story rather than a play. Before reciting some narrative tragedies Chaucer's Monk defined his subject in this way:

> Tragedie is to seyn a certeyn storie,
> As olde bookes maken us memorie,
> Of hym that stood in greet prosperitee,

And is yfallen out of heigh degrèe
Into myserie, and endeth wrecchedly.

. . .

I wol biwaille, in manere of tragedie,
The harm of hem that stoode in heigh degree,
And fillen so that ther nas no remedie
To brynge hem out of hir adversitee.
For certein, whan that Fortune list to flee,
Ther may no man the cours of hire withholde.
Lat no man truste on blynd prosperitee;
Be war by thise ensamples trewe and olde.

The blame for adversity is placed on Fortune, and though this goddess is sometimes conceived of as the executor of God's will, she is commonly considered capricious, turning her wheel to elevate some men and to cast down others who are aloft. Chaucer's tragic figures include men who are totally innocent, such as the noble King Peter of Cyprus, who is slain merely out of envy, the moral being that Fortune can "out of joye bring men to sorwe." The world is mutable and a wise man will reject it: *contemptus mundi,* scorn of the world, is the proper attitude. Something of this attitude is heard near the end of *King Lear,* when Kent speaks of Lear's death as a release from "the rack of this tough world" (V.iii.316). But the Monk's tragic figures include Lucifer, who "fel . . . for his synne," and Adam, who for his "mysgovernaunce/Was dryven out of hys hye prosperitee." Macbeth says something to this effect when he remarks that "even-handed justice/Commends th' ingredients of our poisoned chalice/To our own lips" (I.vii.10–12). These two explanations of the Fall (capricious Fortune or man's vice) continue in later medieval thinking about tragedy and survive into the Renaissance. The title page of *A Mirror for Magistrates* (1559) says that the book shows "with how grievous plagues *vices* are punished; and how frail and unstable worldly prosperity is found, even of those whom *Fortune* seemeth to favor." The dedication says that the book shows "the slippery deceits of the wavering lady [Fortune] and the due reward for all kinds of vice." Sir Philip

Sidney, author of the most important critical treatise of the English Renaissance, similarly observed that tragedy shows both the punishment of vice and "the uncertainty of this world, and upon how weak foundations gilden roofs are builded."

Shakespeare was familiar with the idea of Fortune as arbitrarily casting down those whom she had elevated. A poet in *Timon of Athens* says that his poem tells how "Fortune in her shift and change of mood/Spurns down her late beloved" (I.i. 84–85); Kent says that King Lear is one whom Fortune "loved and hated" (V.iii.283); Richard II sees himself as a character in a book of "sad stories of the death of kings" (III.ii.156). Similarly, Wolsey in *Henry VIII* sees himself as an epitome of mankind, flourishing and then suddenly cut down, and though he goes on to attribute his fall to pride and to equate himself with Lucifer, he implies at the beginning and the end of the speech that the fault is not his:

> Farewell! A long farewell to all my greatness!
> This is the state of man: today he puts forth
> The tender leaves of hopes; tomorrow blossoms,
> And bears his blushing honors thick upon him.
> The third day comes a frost, a killing frost,
> And, when he thinks, good easy man, full surely
> His greatness is aripening, nips his root,
> And then he falls, as I do. I have ventured,
> Like little wanton boys that swim on bladders,
> This many summers in a sea of glory,
> But far beyond my depth. My high-blown pride
> At length broke under me and now has left me,
> Weary and old with service, to the mercy
> Of a rude stream that must forever hide me.
> Vain pomp and glory of this world, I hate ye.
> I feel my heart new opened. O, how wretched
> Is that poor man that hangs on princes' favors!
> There is betwixt that smile we would aspire to,
> That sweet aspect of princes, and their ruin,
> More pangs and fears than wars or women have.
> And when he falls, he falls like Lucifer,
> Never to hope again.   (III.ii.351–72)

What attitude is the spectator to have toward the fall of Shakespeare's tragic heroes? J. V. Cunningham in *Woe or Wonder* convincingly suggests that our response to the tragic action should be guided by Horatio's words in *Hamlet* when he tells Fortinbras and other late arrivals what to make of the sight of the corpses on the stage:

> What is it you would see?
> If aught of woe or wonder, cease your search.   (V.ii.364–65)

"Woe," or pity and fear; "wonder," or astonishment and admiration. The spectacle is all of these, as it would not be if the hero were merely the victim of Fortune or, on the other hand, the victim of his own vice. Shakespeare's tragic heroes are not, of course, all of a kind; at one extreme are Romeo and Juliet, who are chiefly presented as victims ("star-crossed lovers"); in the middle perhaps are Lear ("more sinned against than sinning") and, somewhat more guilty, Mark Antony ("his taints and honors/Waged equal with him"); at the other extreme is Macbeth, who is unequivocally an assassin. But there is always some ambiguity: a number of passages in *Romeo and Juliet* suggest that the lovers are undone by their own haste, or to put it more negatively, by their rashness; at the opposite extreme there is at least the hint that Macbeth is beguiled into evil by the witches and is thus himself a victim of mysterious cosmic forces.

Thus the old idea that Shakespeare's heroes suffer because of a tragic "flaw" is grossly inadequate. In fact, the heroes are sometimes undone by their eminence rather than by their weakness, and to this degree tragic drama is a commemoration of heroism. Some of Shakespeare's tragic heroes have a greatness of spirit that propels them to act, and action increases a man's vulnerability, for it sets up reactions. For example, Hamlet, unable to accept the death of his father and the remarriage of his mother, which the rest of the court (including his mother) accepts easily, stands apart from the court by virtue of his heightened moral sense, and he comes to feel that "The time is out of joint" and that he must set it right. Moreover, Hamlet's death is most immediately brought about not

by any fault (such as the procrastination he is often accused
of) but by his noblemindedness, which does not allow him to
suspect that Laertes will behave treacherously in the duel.
Claudius knows that Hamlet's excellence makes him vulner-
able, and he explains this to Laertes: because he is "Most generous and free from all contriving," Hamlet "Will not peruse
the foils (IV.vii.135–36). Similarly, Othello is brought to murder Desdemona not simply because he is jealous but because
he is (as Iago knows) "of a free and open nature/That thinks
men honest that but seem to be so" (I.iii.388–89). Iago knows,
too, that he can turn Desdemona's "virtue into pitch,/And out
of her own goodness make the net/That shall enmesh them
all" (II.iii.357–59). Excellence, paradoxically, plays its role in
destroying the heroes, for it impels them (as ordinary men are
not impelled) to perform daring actions that have woeful consequences, or it allows lesser men to prey upon them. Those
puritanical critics who denounced tragedies because they were
full of "killing, hewing, stabbing, dagger-drawing, fighting,
butchery, treachery, villainy, etc., and all kinds of heroic evils
whatever" (the words are John Greene's, in 1615) were not un-
fair in their descriptions of the tragic plots, and their indignation suggests not that they failed to see the moral implications
of tragedy but that they clearly saw them and did not like
them. It is, after all, subversive of established morality to suggest that goodness may involve one in evildoing.

   It has been mentioned that in the tragic world actions have
consequences that are irreversible—the most obvious consequences being the deaths that regularly occur near the ends of
the tragedies. (In the comic world, wicked plots fail, and mistakes, such as Puck's anointing of the wrong lover's eyes, can be
reversed.) Claudius poisons Hamlet Senior, Lear gives away his
kingdom, Macbeth hears a prophecy, and great consequences
ensue. Rosencrantz knows that "the cess of majesty" (the death
of a king) is more than the death of an individual:

> The cess of majesty
> Dies not alone, but like a gulf doth draw
> What's near it with it; or it is a massy wheel

Fixed on the summit of the highest mount,
To whose huge spokes ten thousand lesser things
Are mortised and adjoined, which when it falls,
Each small annexment, petty consequence,
Attends the boist'rous ruin. Never alone
Did the king sigh, but with a general groan.

(*Hamlet,* III.iii.15–23)

But this tragic vision of a world in which all events are en-
meshed is complemented by another vision, that of the hero
as becoming progressively isolated. In the course of their suffering and deprivation that will lead to the ultimate deprivation, Shakespeare's tragic heroes usually move away from society. Even at the start, of course, their eminence separates
them in some degree from the rest of mankind, but by and
large (except for Hamlet) they are attached to society: Titus,
Othello, Macbeth, and Coriolanus are indispensable military
leaders, and Lear is a reigning monarch. Their actions, however, propel them into a private world; thus Lear is led to "ab-
jure all roofs" and to move to the stormy heath (II.iv.205), and
Macbeth finds that he can confide in no one, not even in his
wife (III.ii.45). Juliet, isolated from Romeo, from her parents,
and from her Nurse, knows that "My dismal scene I needs
must act alone" (IV.iii.19). Hamlet even at the outset is es-
tranged, and his isolation is increased by the breach between
himself and Ophelia and is then made physical by the sea voyage he is sent on. There are, of course, some partial contacts—
Hamlet with Horatio, Lear with the Fool and Mad Tom and
later with Cordelia—but even these contacts only serve to emphasize the terrible inner isolation of the tragic heroes. This
isolation normally produces in the tragic hero a new sense of
identity; thrown back upon himself, he comes to see more
clearly what he is. Before his journey to the heath, Lear feels
his identity crumbling when, astounded by his daughters' ingratitude, he asks,

Does any here know me? This is not Lear.
Does Lear walk thus? Speak thus? Where are his eyes?

Who is it that can tell me who I am?　　　(I.iv.227–28, 231)

On the heath Lear gets to know who he is; he is one who has "ta'en/Too little care."

> Poor naked wretches, wheresoe'er you are,
> That bide the pelting of this pitiless storm,
> How shall your houseless heads and unfed sides,
> Your looped and windowed raggedness, defend you
> From seasons such as these? O, I have ta'en
> Too little care of this! Take physic, pomp;
> Expose thyself to feel what wretches feel.   (III.iv.28–34)

Similarly, Macbeth comes to the recognition (Aristotle's term is *anagnorisis*) that his earlier actions have had a result opposite from that which he intended. He aimed at the crown, thinking it would bring him happiness, but his hopes deceived him:

> I have lived long enough. My way of life
> Is fall'n into the sear, the yellow leaf,
> And that which should accompany old age,
> As honor, love, obedience, troops of friends,
> I must not look to have; but, in their stead,
> Curses not loud but deep, mouth-honor, breath,
> Which the poor heart would fain deny, and dare not.
>
> (V.iii.22–28)

Behind these articulate recognitions—and very far behind them in quality though not in date—are the confessions or addresses to the world made by characters in *A Mirror for Magistrates*.

Before pursuing the literary background of Shakespeare's tragedies, it is well to remember that plays owe something to life as well as to literature. The Renaissance believed in heroes—men who, conscious of their greatness, were moved to do great deeds. A single example must suffice: in 1591 Sir Richard Grenville, an English admiral, refused to flee from the Spaniards, taking on their fleet for fifteen hours. When all was lost, he ordered the master gunner to blow up his ship in order to avoid capture. The crew, however, not seeing themselves as heroes, refused. Grenville, though treated courteously by his Spanish captors, is said to have then seized the first opportunity to commit suicide: he crushed his wine glass and ate the pieces. His dying words reportedly were, "Here die I, Richard Grenville, with a joyful and quiet mind, for that I have ended my life as a true soldier ought to do that hath fought for his country, queen, religion, and honor."

But of course there are also dramatic traditions behind Shakespeare's tragedies. Though neither the miracle play nor the morality play (see pp. 33–37) is tragic, both forms contributed to Elizabethan tragedy. The miracle play sometimes deals with tyrants such as Pharaoh and Herod, showing their cruelty and the punishment subsequently visited upon them, and in its later development it deals also with the tribulations of saints. The morality play regularly dramatizes the conflict of vice and virtue, and it often dramatizes the coming of death, sometimes conceiving of death as retribution for sin. The villains in these plays contributed to the making of the Elizabethan villain. Biblical tyrants of the miracle plays doubtless exerted an influence on the secular tyrants of mid-sixteenth-century "conqueror" plays, and so did such a figure as the wicked prince in *The Cradle of Security* (see pp. 36–37); the innocent sufferers of the miracle plays and the representatives of fallible mankind in the morality plays also exerted an influence on the Elizabethan tragic hero, but none of these characters are Shakespearean tragic heroes.

Another dramatic tradition, derived from the Roman dramatist Seneca, helped to give Elizabethan tragedy its characteristic "woe," though as we have already seen, woe was the keynote of medieval nondramatic tragic writing. Greek tragedy was little known, but in university circles at least Seneca (4 B.C.?–65 A.D.) was widely known, though perhaps more for his moral philosophy than for his plays. Nonetheless, from about the middle of the sixteenth century onward Seneca's plays were translated; the first English translation was published in 1559, the year of the first edition of *A Mirror for Magistrates*. Academic authors sometimes imitated Seneca's plays, and these imitations exerted an influence on the popular dramatists, some of whom were university graduates and all of whom could at least read Seneca in translation. That he was read in translation is indicated by Thomas Nashe's assertion in 1589 that "English Seneca read by candlelight yields many good sentences, as 'Blood is a beggar.' " (An English writer who wanted to make some use of Seneca did not have to read any of Seneca's books. He could turn to a collection of classical quotations; from such a collection he would learn nothing about Seneca's plays as a whole, but he would get some suitable moral sentiments.) Seneca's two chief themes are tyranny and revenge (both of which appear conspicuously in Shakespeare's *Titus Andronicus, Richard III, Julius Caesar,* and *Hamlet*); his characters are fiercely passionate and given to alternating between furious denunciations and stoic meditations (one thinks of Hamlet and of the Player's denunciation of "strumpet Fortune" in II.ii, which is surely in the Elizabethan Senecan mode); and the prevailing atmosphere is one of horror, rather like Hamlet's "the very witching time of night,/When churchyards yawn, and hell itself breathes out/ Contagion to this world." Certainly an Elizabethan playwright did not have to go to Seneca's plays for any of these themes, but the very fact that they were already a part of the English tradition perhaps made Seneca the more accessible and the more welcome: here was a classical playwright whose use of such material gave it an added dignity. Seneca helped the playwrights of the decades before Shakespeare to draw upon history and legendary history, showing the fall of tyrants and the suffering visited upon passionate heroes rather than upon the character abstractions of the morality play. Moreover, when in the 1580's—and perhaps even in the 1570's—the playwrights turned to continental stories (*novelle*) for material, they could by a somewhat Senecan treatment elevate to a tragic status these tales, which for the most part dealt either with the pathetic deaths of innocent lovers in a world of intrigue or with crime and vengeance. Again, this is not to say that Seneca was responsible for the character of Elizabethan tragedy; without the help of Seneca John Bale had already adapted the political morality play into a play showing the fall of an historical figure, King John, though Bale retained some abstractions. Even Sackville and Norton's *Gorboduc* (1561), the first English historical play without moral abstractions, praised by Sir Philip Sidney for "climbing to the height of Seneca his style," is deeply indebted to the morality play in its treatment of the good and wicked counselors who flank the king and in its heavy emphasis on the moral implications of action. Seneca, however, did not merely provide aphorisms of the sort Nashe alluded to; he also gave a classical sanction to the depictions of great falls due not simply to Fortune (though the fickleness of Fortune is one of his motifs) but to passionate natures that in some measure destroy themselves and to the revenge plot urged by a ghost (though there are only two ghosts in Seneca's plays, that of Tantalus in *Thyestes* and that of Thyestes in *Agamemnon*). Of course, the Elizabethans, influenced by earlier episodic drama and by Italian fictions of intrigue, regularly complicated this plot far more than Seneca did (his plots begin just before the catastrophe, and his plays are largely dramatizations of a hero contemplating his suffering), and they often added to the revenge plot other matter—for example, comic scenes—that was un-Senecan but thoroughly in the medieval dramatic tradition. Hamlet tells us that for the players who come to Elsinore "Seneca cannot be too heavy" (II.ii. 407). Seneca was, in fact, too heavy for the English popular theater, which preferred "mongrel tragicomedy," but he provided the dramatists with moral tags and motifs, and with a respectable model if they cared to look for one. What they saw in Seneca, of course, was what they wanted to see. *Titus Andronicus* does not closely resemble any play by Seneca (though it quotes from him), but Shakespeare probably felt that in it he had written an appropriately classical play.

THREE EARLY TRAGEDIES:
TITUS ANDRONICUS, ROMEO AND JULIET, JULIUS CAESAR

Like *The Comedy of Errors* (probably Shakespeare's first comedy), *Titus Andronicus* is very much an academic play. In Ovid, the Roman nondramatic poet whom he had read in school, Shakespeare found the prettified violent story of Philomela, which is explicitly referred to in *Titus* (IV.i.42 ff.) and which resembles parts of Shakespeare's plot. From Seneca (or from English Senecan plays such as Thomas Kyd's *The Spanish Tragedy*) Shakespeare derived the motif of a hero who, unable to get justice from the state, is driven to madness and to feigning madness, and who finally exacts a terrible revenge. The author of *Titus Andronicus* advertises his bookishness not only by the numerous mythological references and declamatory passages but by an explicit reference to William Lily's Latin grammar, the text used in grammar schools throughout Elizabethan England. One of Titus' enemies says of a Latin message attached to a bundle of weapons:

> O, 'tis a verse in Horace; I know it well:
> I read it in the grammar long ago.   (IV.ii.22–23)

The rather symmetrical arrangements of the characters in *Titus*—loving brothers and quarreling brothers, a virgin and a mistress, and so on—also suggest a playwright who is anxious to do things properly. But if the characters are sometimes too neatly paired, a heritage from the morality play, and if they often seem to recite rather than to talk to each other, there is still a good deal of subtlety in the play. For example, Titus, the inflexibly honorable and somewhat simple general, is contrasted not only with Aaron, the cunning villain, but with Marcus, Titus' humane brother. There is scarcely a scene or a character that does not in some way echo or contrast with another scene or character, and although these echoes and contrasts are often a bit obvious, they are nonetheless the very stuff of tragedy, where every action has its consequences—where, as Alfred North Whitehead said, we see "the remorseless working of things." Titus believes that honor requires him to sacrifice to his dead sons a son of his enemy; he acts on this belief, and thus he inevitably evokes the enmity of the victim's mother, who retaliates with outrages upon Titus' children, thereby goading Titus into counterretaliation. The elaborate parallelisms in *Titus*, then, are not very different from those in the later and greater tragedies; they are simply more obvious. In *Hamlet*, for example, the protagonist is flanked by Laertes and Fortinbras, each of whom (like Hamlet) has lost a father; in *King Lear* the protagonist is flanked by wicked daughters and a good daughter, and Gloucester has a wicked son and a good son. But the symmetry of *Titus*, though obvious, is by no means naive, and Shakespeare never discarded the technique. Moreover, it is not wholly illegitimate to read back into *Titus* characters and scenes from *Othello* (the Machiavellian Aaron anticipates Iago in his scheming, and the honest soldier Titus anticipates Othello), from *Hamlet* (driven to revenge, Titus is both mad and playing at madness), and from *King Lear* (Titus is driven beyond the bounds of sanity). And in IV.iii the first of the clowns in Shakespeare's tragedies appears; his role is minute, but he would have been unthinkable in one of Seneca's plays, and we are grateful for this simple voice that sounds across the rhetoric of the heroic (and villainous) world. We are grateful, too, that even in this savage play we hear the voice of sympathy that we come to feel is characteristic of Shakespeare's prevailing vision: in III.i a messenger, carrying Titus' severed hand and the heads of two of Titus' sons, concludes his speech to Titus with a note of sympathy that we cherish:

> Woe is me to think upon thy woes,
> More than remembrance of my father's death.   (III.i.239–40)

(Such generosity is not the messenger's alone; it is Shakespeare's, who pays mankind the compliment of assuming that one man's sorrow touches another man's heart.) Finally, like most of Shakespeare's other tragedies, *Titus* has affinities with political concerns. It begins with matters of political succession and concludes with the suggestion that the state, which has undergone a convulsion more or less parallel to the anguish of the tragic hero, will be reunited.

What does not appear in *Titus*, however, is the achievement of self-understanding characteristic of the later tragic heroes. Titus sees Rome (aptly enough) as a "wilderness of tigers"

(III.i.54), but he does not see the barbarity of his own inflexible code of honor, which Tamora accurately enough characterizes as a "cruel, irreligious piety" (I.i.130). Titus sees only the enemy outside himself; he never enters upon the sort of prolonged examination of his own actions that leads King Lear to say, "I have ta'en/Too little care of this."

Romeo and Juliet (1594–96) was preceded not only by *Titus* but by some history plays with tragic aspects and, no less important for the present purpose, by at least two comedies about lovers, one of which, like *Romeo and Juliet,* is set in Verona. Probably, too, Shakespeare was writing his sonnets at this time. Thus he was developing as a poet of love, and it is not surprising that he then turned to a tragedy of love. More exactly, it is not surprising to us; but an Elizabethan audience was probably surprised to find lovers—rather than heroic figures—the subject of a tragedy. Love was the stuff of comedies, and only a few earlier tragedies deal with love, though continental fiction offered many tales of young lovers destroyed by a cruel world. *Romeo and Juliet* was written at about the time of *Richard II* and *A Midsummer Night's Dream* (the exact dates are unknown); like these two other plays, *Romeo and Juliet* is conspicuously lyrical. For example, there is a sonnet in the dialogue between Romeo and Juliet, and the sonnet uses the conventional poetic figure of the lover as a pilgrim:

ROMEO
If I profane with my unworthiest hand
  This holy shrine, the gentle sin is this:
My lips, two blushing pilgrims, ready stand
  To smooth that rough touch with a tender kiss.

JULIET
Good pilgrim, you do wrong your hand too much,
  Which mannerly devotion shows in this;
For saints have hands that pilgrims' hands do touch,
  And palm to palm is holy palmers' kiss.

ROMEO
Have not saints lips, and holy palmers too?

JULIET
Ay, pilgrim, lips that they must use in prayer.

ROMEO
O, then, dear saint, let lips do what hands do!
They pray; grant thou, lest faith turn to despair.

JULIET
Saints do not move, though grant for prayers' sake.

ROMEO
Then move not while my prayer's effect I take.

[*Kisses her.*]   (I.v.95–108)

Moreover, like its near-contemporary *Richard II*, the play is
rich in iterative imagery, recurrent images that help to define
its meaning. In *Romeo and Juliet* there are abundant images
of a speed that soon exhausts itself and of light yielding to
darkness, both of which are appropriate in a play about the
early death of two ardent lovers surrounded by enmity. For
example:

Wisely and slow. They stumble that run fast.   (II.iii.94)

These violent delights have violent ends
And in their triumph die, like fire and powder,
Which, as they kiss, consume.   (II.vi.9–11)

Such imagery helps to suggest the naturalness or inevitability
of the lovers' deaths. The inevitability is also directly asserted
by the Chorus, which speaks of the "star-crossed lovers," and
this motif is periodically repeated, as when Romeo says,

                    My mind misgives
Some consequence yet hanging in the stars
Shall bitterly begin his fearful date
With this night's revels.   (I.iv.106–09)

The emphasis on the feud between the families also suggests
that overpowering forces surround the lovers. Thus if we can
look at the tragedy as proceeding in part from the passion of
the lovers, we can also look at it as proceeding in part from the
forces of destiny. That is, we can see the characters as contrib-
uting to their downfall, and we can also see them as victims.
Juliet's father, in the play's penultimate speech, remembering
the feud that has forced the lovers to a fatal secrecy, calls them

"poor sacrifices of our enmity," thus emphasizing the suggestion that Romeo and Juliet are martyred victims. Shakespeare probably saw the play as appropriately classical in spirit: Seneca's emphasis on the blows of Fortune (Romeo sees himself as "fortune's fool") is translated into both dire astrological influence and chance (Romeo does not receive the letter sent to inform him that Juliet has taken a potion); and like a Senecan hero Romeo is occasionally stoical ("I defy you, stars"). Some of the hyperboles ("chain me. with roaring bears") have a Senecan ring; and the long final scene, set in a tomb, with its talk of worms as Juliet's chambermaids, and with the bloody corpse of Paris lying nearby, would probably have brought approving nods from university men. On the other hand, the play is distinctly un-Senecan in its hero, in its bustle, and in its comedy. The quarreling servants at the outset give a comic treatment of the feud, suggesting its tragic possibilities; the bawdy comments of Mercutio and the Nurse are delightful in themselves (or would be, if we did not need explanatory footnotes), yet they are also integral in this play about love.

When he turned to his third tragedy, *Julius Caesar* (1599–1600), Shakespeare had already also written nine plays on English history and about half a dozen comedies. In the histories Shakespeare explores the unending political developments that press on from one play to the next; on the whole the concern is with man as a political rather than moral creature, with what *happened* rather than (as in tragedy) with what *happens*. (Two of the history plays, however, *Richard III* and *Richard II,* have affinities with tragedy; though *Richard III* is closer to melodrama than to tragedy, *Richard II* gives us a hero whose fall is rooted in character as well as in bad luck. But *Richard II* is a history play rather than a tragedy because political concerns are consistently present and also because interest in Richard's fall is balanced by interest in Bolingbroke's rise.) After completing *Henry V* Shakespeare may have felt that he had exhausted English history, for he had already written on the reign of Henry VI, and to continue beyond the reign of Henry VI would have brought him, in effect, to the origins of contemporary politics—in short, too close to present matters. In any case, around 1599 Shakespeare turned to Roman history, writing a play that, like those on English history, concerns political machinations; but in Brutus he explores more fully a man making a moral decision and then suffering its consequences. (Julius Caesar, like Henry IV in the two plays named for him, is the center of all forces in the play and, like Henry IV, he is not the protagonist.) *Julius Caesar* owes something to Shakespeare's earlier history plays, which were at least occasionally concerned with the idea of retributive justice, and its structure owes something to 2 *Henry VI* (see the discussion of that play); and it of course owes something to earlier Elizabethan tragedies, which showed a downfall, but it differs from those tragedies in an important way: in Brutus, Shakespeare presents the fall neither of a tyrant nor of a weakling but of a noble yet flawed hero, a man who seeks to act for his country's good. Shakespeare's English histories are not greatly concerned with moral crises; nor do his two earlier tragedies indicate much concern of this sort. In *Romeo and Juliet* the lovers do not greatly ponder their course of action; they are overwhelmingly in love, and they are "star-crossed," but in *Julius Caesar* at least to a large degree "the fault . . . is not in our stars,/But in ourselves." Brutus tries to live according to a moral code, pondering a course of action, coming to a conclusion, acting (there is, by the way, something of an anticipation of Hamlet here, especially in Brutus' introspection), and then suffering the unexpected yet, to our view, inevitable consequences of the action. Ironically, too, Brutus falls into evil and ultimately into destruction largely because of his nobility: had he been less high-minded and more worldly minded, more politically sophisticated, Cassius could not have manipulated him so easily. Cassius makes this point clear in a soliloquy:

> Well, Brutus, thou art noble; yet I see
> Thy honorable mettle may be wrought
> From that it is disposed; therefore it is meet
> That noble minds keep ever with their likes.   (I.ii.306–09)

And so Cassius can win Brutus to the conspiracy by forging letters that flatter Brutus. Still, Brutus is not quite so noble as Cassius and Brutus think. Brutus deludes himself by believing that his quarrel is with "ambition," not with Caesar, and that in the assassination of Caesar he and his fellows are "sacrificers, but not butchers." Moreover, though Brutus' pursuit of virtue is admirable, there is something disconcerting and stuffy in his pride; although we place him morally above Cassius, we cannot wholly admire him. Cassius himself, however, is not the cunning, successful man-of-the-world that he thinks he is, for he too is destroyed, and by his own hand, when he commits suicide in the mistaken belief that the battle is lost. The successful man in the play is Antony, who is adept at manipulating people, most notably in his funeral oration in III.ii. He is not a villain, but insofar as he works on others he is an ancestor of such arch-villains as Edmund in *King Lear* and Iago in *Othello*. These later voices are anticipated in Antony's wry, self-satisfied comment in the middle of the play, when he sees that he has moved the plebeians to fury:

> Now let it work: Mischief, thou art afoot,
> Take thou what course thou wilt.   (III.ii.261–62)

Of course, like Brutus, Caesar too is a tragic figure. It seems clear that Shakespeare saw him as fitting the tragic formula of a man who falls from a great height. He has been blamed for his arrogance, and indeed he is unlovely, though we may wonder if we would prefer just before his assassination a less supremely confident figure, a man who (for example) eagerly clutched at Artemidorus' warning message instead of brushing it off with "What touches us ourself shall be last served" (III.i.7). Caesar is arrogant, subject to flattery, and petty, but despite his faults he is a hero, "great Caesar," shrewd, dignified (at times), theatrical, and powerful. As a comparison with Plutarch's life of Caesar indicates, Shakespeare was careful to omit some of Caesar's most ignoble actions. Moreover, he gave Caesar an added dignity just prior to the assassination by virtue of his cordiality to the conspirators ("Good friends, go in and taste some wine with me"), and especially by virtue of the lies and the fawning that the conspirators engage in when they surround Caesar. Finally, there is the pathos of "Et tu, Bruté? Then fall Caesar," when the wounded leader perceives that his trust in Brutus was misplaced. The play, then, is concerned with two tragic figures (a third, if we wish to add Cassius).

Julius Caesar is concerned with political problems to a much greater degree than the later tragedies are; the rather "public" or "Roman" tone, found even in the soliloquies, where the characters look at themselves as objectively as possible and sometimes even speak of themselves in the third person, contributes to our sense that Shakespeare is concerned with abstractions as well as with people. But this play nevertheless shows Shakespeare moving toward the complexities of the later tragedies, in which the tragic characters act and then must face the ironic consequences of their action. What we do not get in *Julius Caesar* is much sense of characters developing a profound awareness of themselves through suffering. They tend to be static (doubtless this was part of Shakespeare's conception of heroic Romans), and the closest we come to a tragic recognition or *anagnorisis* is Cassius' "Caesar, thou art revenged,/Even with the sword that killed thee" (V.iii. 45–46) and Brutus' words on his own suicide, "Caesar, now be still;/I killed not thee with half so good a will" (V.v.50–51).

THE LATER TRAGEDIES:
HAMLET, OTHELLO, KING LEAR, MACBETH,
ANTONY AND CLEOPATRA, CORIOLANUS

As usual, the dates of the later tragedies are uncertain, but apparently between 1600 and 1608 Shakespeare wrote *Hamlet, Othello, King Lear, Macbeth, Antony and Cleopatra,* and *Coriolanus.* In these years, too, he probably wrote his two "dark" comedies, *All's Well That Ends Well* and *Measure for Measure,* a markedly ironic tragedy, *Troilus and Cressida,* and a play about a notorious misanthrope, *Timon of Athens.*

The conjunction of these plays has sometimes caused readers to assume that Shakespeare entered a "tragic" period, a period of despair during which he poured out his heart in tragic, dark, and bitter plays while he underwent a mental crisis. The crisis has been variously identified as the failure of Essex' revolution in 1601; Shakespeare's father's death in 1601; and an unsuccessful love affair, described in the sonnets concerning the Dark Lady, on whom Shakespeare had his revenge in his portraits of Cressida and Cleopatra. (But, we might ask, how do we account for Cordelia and "the divine Desdemona"?) Such views, however, assume that an author writes tragedy when he is depressed, and they do not give adequate weight to the fact that tragedy was an established literary genre at which Shakespeare had earlier tried his hand in *Titus, Romeo and Juliet,* and *Julius Caesar.* Perhaps, then, it is best to see the great tragedies as the achievement of mastery in a genre rather than as veiled autobiography.

Hamlet, Shakespeare's first great tragedy, is the most widely quoted, most often alluded to, and most often written about of Shakespeare's plays. The abundance of commentary, however, stems in part from uncertainties that are found in the play, and T. S. Eliot was not alone in suggesting that *Hamlet* is an artistic failure. Why does Hamlet delay? Because he must confirm the report of the Ghost, who may be a devil? Because he is a coward? Because his moral code disapproves of killing? Because he cannot kill the man who fulfilled Hamlet's unconscious Oedipal wish to kill his own father? Inevitably another question arises: *Does* Hamlet delay? He says he does, but some critics have argued that he merely chastises himself needlessly or, alternatively, that Shakespeare was merely creating a spurious suspense by reminding us of what still had to be done. (In any case, it is obvious that in a play dealing with revenge there inevitably would be an interval between the action that causes a desire for vengeance and the fulfilling of this vengeance.) Yet another question: Is Hamlet mad or only pretending to be? (Oscar Wilde varied the question: Are the commentators on *Hamlet* mad or only pretending to be?)

In the 1580's playwrights had linked Senecan motifs of

passion and revenge with continental stories of intrigue, notably in Thomas Kyd's *The Spanish Tragedy*. Almost surely there was a play about Hamlet before Shakespeare's, perhaps by Kyd, and this Hamlet was apparently conspicuous for his cunning, his madness, and his savagery. Shakespeare's Hamlet in some degree shares these traits—enough so that George Bernard Shaw complained that Hamlet kills three people and is forever apologizing that he hasn't killed a fourth. There is something to this view. Hamlet mistakenly kills Polonius, and his chief reaction is regret that his victim was not Claudius. He forges orders so that Rosencrantz and Guildenstern will be "put to sudden death,/Not shriving time allowed" (V.ii. 46–47), though Rosencrantz and Guildenstern are merely serving the man who they have every reason to suppose is their lawful king. Hamlet has no regrets about dispatching these two men: "They are not near my conscience" (V.ii.58). Consider, too, his rough verbal treatment of Ophelia and of his mother, and his desire not only to kill Claudius but to damn his soul (III.iii.73–96). But this, of course, is not the whole story, and Hamlet has not lacked for sympathizers. According to Goethe's Wilhelm Meister, Hamlet, "a lovely, pure, noble and most moral nature, without the strength of nerve which forms a hero, sinks beneath a burden which it cannot bear and must not cast away."

Perhaps both of these views, and others, have some merit; perhaps, too, Hamlet changes as the play goes on, from (to put it crudely) a revenger full of anguish, self-hatred, and fury —not at all surprising in a world mined with "rank corruption"—to an avenger who comes to see that his job is not to set the world right or to devise a trap wherein he can catch Claudius' soul but to be an instrument of God's will. In III.ii he praises Horatio for his dispassionateness, saying that Horatio "is not passion's slave." But in III.iii, when Hamlet, in a position to kill the praying king, announces that he will delay until he can catch Claudius in a sinful act, we see clearly how hideous a *dis*passionate revenge would be. Here, if anywhere, Hamlet repels us. But late in the play, after his return from the sea voyage, he seems to have changed: he is courteous to the gravediggers, and in V.ii he apologizes to Laertes. (Speaking of Laertes, it is worth mentioning that Laertes is an active young man who sweeps to his revenge, as some critics suggest Hamlet should. Hamlet spares the king at prayer, but Laertes says he would cut his foe's throat in church; and Laertes will not scruple to use a poisoned foil. Yet there cannot be any doubt that Hamlet, despite his scruples—perhaps because of his scruples—is the more heroic figure. The contrast with Fortinbras in IV.iv works similarly: Hamlet thinks that Fortinbras is brave and resolute in his war against Poland, but even through Hamlet's praise of Fortinbras—a man who will risk life to "all that fortune, death, and danger dare,/Even for an eggshell"—we can perceive the limitations of action and the difficulty and superiority of reflectiveness in a corrupt world.) Most important, after his return from the sea voyage, Hamlet has ceased to be an intriguer and is content to be an instrument: "We defy augury. There is special providence in the fall of a sparrow. . . . The readiness is all" (V.ii.221–24). Of course there are complications here too, and critics have sometimes wondered whether Hamlet, who at first has such trouble bringing himself to act, does not ultimately lapse into a sluggish fatalism. Possibly this is true, though Christian resignation, based on hope, faith, and charity, is hardly the same as Stoic fatalism; and in any case we probably prefer a sluggish Hamlet to a scheming one. The rest of the play—his manly duel with Laertes, his execution of justice on Claudius, Laertes' tribute to "noble Hamlet," and Fortinbras' testimonial and the military funeral—suggests that Hamlet's course is noble.

Despite the variety of interpretations, it must be agreed that Shakespeare's dramaturgy is unerring: those who want patterns of imagery (notably concerning war, sickness, the nature of action, and appearance versus reality) can find them; those who want rounded characters (sometimes established by contrasts with other characters, as Hamlet is contrasted with Laertes and Fortinbras) can find them; those who want philosophic poetic speeches and earthy prose speeches can find them; and those who want suspense, and then the fulfillment of expectations, can find it: the opening scene, for example, begins—appropriately for a play that has puzzled so many—with a question, "Who's there?" The suspense is then skillfully built up, slackened, and built up again with "this thing," "this dreaded sight," and "this apparition," and finally (still only at line 39) the Ghost appears, even as a previous appearance is being described. It disappears and is discussed, and during a long speech about the uncertain military situation (which introduces a reference to Caesar's ghost) it reappears, and again vanishes as the cock crows, evoking lyrical speeches from Marcellus and Horatio that help to diminish the uncertainty by introducing thoughts of purification, partly explicitly Christian (I.i.158–61) and partly natural (I.i.166–67). And so in 170 lines the scene changes from midnight to dawn (in the first 40 lines we are told eleven times that it is night), and the play moves from a sense of fear and mysterious anguish (beginning with Francisco's "I am sick at heart") to hope. The meaning of the play may baffle us, but the artistry of the play can only convince us that Shakespeare had perfected his skill, and it is not at all surprising that he went on to write other tragedies.

Hamlet has a complicated plot (there is intrigue and counterintrigue, and a subplot concerning Fortinbras) and a philosophically minded protagonist who calls into doubt the nature of action. *Othello,* Shakespeare's next tragedy, is simpler on both accounts: the plot is derived from an Italian short story and can be summarized in a few sentences, and the nature of the events is never called into doubt. A. C. Bradley put it thus: "*Othello* has not . . . the power of dilating the imagination by vague suggestions of huge universal powers working in the world of individual fate and passion." If we are attentive to the hero's hyperboles, and to the villain's diabolical malice (see p. 56), we do hear some suggestions of "universal powers," but in the main Bradley is right. There are no soothsayers, ghosts, omens, or witches (despite Brabantio's charges) to draw our attention to a world larger than the characters' social world. And though Othello is a great military hero, his fate does not greatly affect the entire world around him, as, say, Hamlet's does.

Perhaps because the play is at least superficially rather simple and its hero is said to be "noble," much twentieth-century criticism, unhappy with simplicity and nobility, has found the play wanting, or has complicated it by suggesting (for example) that Othello is not what he seems to be. The critical tendency to diminish Othello—to see him as immature and theatrical if not corrupt—is perhaps best known in T. S. Eliot's comment on Othello's penultimate speech, which Eliot characterizes as an "exposure of human weakness." Eliot's point is that the speech is not to be taken at face value; rather, Eliot says, Othello should be viewed as "cheering himself up. He is endeavoring to escape reality, he has ceased to think about Desdemona and is thinking about himself. . . . Othello . . . [is] adopting an *aesthetic* rather than a moral attitude." Here is the speech; it is exactly the same length (eighteen and a half lines) as his first address to the Senate (I.iii.76–94), and it conveys his old dignity as he delivers again "a round unvarnished tale."

> Soft you, a word or two before you go.
> I have done the state some service, and they know't.
> No more of that. I pray you, in your letters,
> When you shall these unlucky deeds relate,
> Speak of me as I am. Nothing extenuate,
> Nor set down aught in malice. Then must you speak
> Of one that loved not wisely, but too well;
> Of one not easily jealous, but, being wrought,
> Perplexed in the extreme; of one whose hand,
> Like the base Judean, threw a pearl away
> Richer than all his tribe; of one whose subdued eyes,
> Albeit unusèd to the melting mood,
> Drops tears as fast as the Arabian trees
> Their med'cinable gum. Set you down this.
> And say besides that in Aleppo once,
> Where a malignant and a turbaned Turk
> Beat a Venetian and traduced the state,
> I took by th' throat the circumcisèd dog

And smote him—thus.

    [*He stabs himself.*]   (V.ii.337–55)

Against Eliot's view it can be argued that Othello judges himself accurately and severely: he compares himself to a Turk (in this play, repeatedly designated the enemy of Christian civilization), and he inflicts upon himself the same punishment that he inflicted on the Turkish enemy. Having recaptured his faith in Desdemona, recognized his responsibility for her death, and condemned and executed himself, like Romeo and Mark Antony he pays his beloved a last tribute of a kiss, affirming his faith in her value, uniting himself with her, and demonstrating that Iago has not, finally, corrupted him.

It seems appropriate to move from *Hamlet* and *Othello* directly to *King Lear* (though possibly *Timon of Athens* was written between these two plays), for *Lear* seems to be displacing *Hamlet* as the play that speaks to our time. *Hamlet* was especially popular with nineteenth-century critics, who often found in the uncertain prince an image of their own doubts in a world in which belief in a benevolent divine order was collapsing under the influence of scientific materialism and bourgeois aggressiveness. Many critics in our age find in *Lear*—where "for many miles about/There's scarce a bush" —a play thoroughly in the spirit of *Waiting for Godot,* where the scenery consists of a single tree. *Lear* has the amplitude that Bradley found lacking in *Othello,* and it is terrifying. Moreover, does not Lear denounce the hypocrisy of the power structure and expose the powerlessness of the disenfranchised? "Robes and furred gowns hide all. Plate sin with gold,/And the strong lance of justice hurtless breaks;/Arm it in rags, a pygmy's straw does pierce it" (IV.vi.165–67). And so Lear strips off his clothing (III.iv) and reduces himself to "a poor, bare, forked animal," to find the essential man, "the thing itself." Is there no more? What of the gods? The characters in the play offer various comments on the government of the universe, ranging from "As flies to wanton boys, are we to th' gods,/They kill us for their sport" (IV.i.36–37) to "The gods are just" (V.iii.172). But perhaps the most memorable reference to the gods is not a mere comment but a comment followed by an action: learning that Cordelia is in danger, Albany cries out, "The gods defend her!" (V.iii.258), and immediately his words are mocked by Lear's entrance on the stage, with the dead Cordelia in his arms.

For Kent, a moment later, "all's cheerless, dark, and deadly," and it almost seems true. But only almost, for the interpretation of *Lear* as a revelation of the emptiness of life fails to consider at least two things. First, there is an affirmation in those passages in which Lear comes to see that he is not what he thought he was. For example:

> They flattered me . . . . When the rain came to wet me once and the wind to make me chatter; when the thunder would not peace at my bidding; there I found 'em, there I smelt 'em out. Go to, they are not men o' their words: they told me I was everything; 'tis a lie, I am not ague-proof [secure against fever].   (IV.vi.96–105)

Second, this *anagnorisis* (or recognition) is several times associated with love or charity, as when Lear with unexpected tenderness invites the Fool to enter the hovel first and then confesses his guilt in having cared too little for humanity (III. iv.26–36). And this care for humanity is seen in Cordelia, who comes—though ineffectually in the long run—to the aid of her father; it is seen too in the nameless servant who at the end of III.vii promises to apply medicine to Gloucester's eyeless sockets; it is seen even in the villainous Edmund, who in dying repents and says, "Some good I mean to do,/Despite of mine own nature" (V.iii.245–46), and who thereupon seeks, unsuccessfully, to save Cordelia. Only a Dr. Pangloss would say that these actions turn *King Lear* into a happy vision, but it is perverse to ignore them, and to refuse to see that in this play love humanizes as surely as egoism dehumanizes.

Finally, then, *King Lear* is a profound morality play; like *Everyman*, Lear is called to account and finds that those he unthinkingly trusted—Goneril and Regan—offer him no help and that those he used most harshly—Kent and Cordelia— minister to him in his trial and present him patterns of love. This is not to say that Lear is purified by suffering and becomes a saint at the end—he can still rage—but it does suggest that if the play dramatizes man's isolation and the potency of evil, it also dramatizes (as the Theater of the Absurd does not) the love that, while providing no protection against pain or death, makes man's life something different from the life of "a dog, a horse, a rat."

In *Macbeth*, Shakespeare forsook the double plot that he used in *King Lear* (the story of Lear and his daughters and the parallel story of Gloucester and his sons) and concentrated, as he had in *Othello*, on a single and simple plot. Like *King Lear*, however, *Macbeth* has its most immediate origin not in a short tale but in Holinshed's *Chronicles*. Like *King Lear*, too, it is reasonably classified as a tragedy rather than as a history (even though it is a descendant of the mid-sixteenth-century moral history plays, and it is, by virtue of the theme of retribution, closely related to *Richard III*) because it is a play more about people than about politics, more about what happens than about what happened. The play is chiefly concerned with Macbeth, much less so with Scottish history. Yet politics are a part of the play: it was written during the reign of James I of England, who was James VI of Scotland; perhaps it was written *for* James, who was regarded as a descendant of Banquo and who therefore is implicitly complimented in the procession of kings and Banquo in IV.i.

The political nature of the play appears too in the strong emphasis at the end on a Scotland purged of evil and guided by a rightful hand. The tragedies regularly end with the suggestion that after the tragic hero's death, order is restored, though this order that the survivors form is pale when compared with the hero's greatness. Thus in *Titus Andronicus* Lucius is acclaimed "Rome's gracious governor" (V.iii.146), and he makes plans to inter the dead and to punish the villain; in *Romeo and Juliet* the feud that divides the city is concluded, though the death of the lovers may well make us feel that the vibrancy has gone out of Verona; in *Julius Caesar* Octavius pays tribute to Brutus and holds the reins of government; in *Hamlet* Fortinbras pays tribute to Hamlet and acquires the Danish throne; in *King Lear* Albany (Lear's son-in-law) invites Edgar to "Rule in this realm and the gored state sustain" (V.iii.322). Thus it is no surprise that at the end of *Macbeth* Malcolm is placed on the throne, promising justice. But because Macbeth is a villain-hero (and because the play was probably designed in part to celebrate King James) the protagonist is unusually diminished—he is "this dead butcher" —and the happy future of the new reign is emphasized. Scotland had suffered great disorder for a while because its murderous ruler was disordered, but now its rightful monarch will order the realm:

> this, and what needful else
> That calls upon us, by the grace of Grace
> We will perform in measure, time, and place:
> So thanks to all at once and to each one,
> Whom we invite to see us crowned at Scone.   (V.viii.71–75)

The choice of a villain-hero probably does not indicate that Shakespeare's sense of human guilt had deepened, and it should be noted that Macbeth is given a measure of sympathy and humanity denied to an earlier villain-hero, Richard III. Richard only briefly, at the end, suffers doubts and fears, and in doing so he becomes less of a medieval Vice figure and more of an Everyman, or simply a terrified, realistic king; but Macbeth's conscience regularly reminds him of his guilt, and he is punished not only at the end by death but throughout by anxiety and sleeplessness. (Lady Macbeth's sleepwalking and her suicide also suggest the pervasiveness of retribution.) Even before Macbeth kills Duncan he is afflicted; but, not knowing himself, he persists, and when he achieves his ambition of ascending the throne (Act III opens with "Thou hast it now: king"), he learns that the prize is torment:

> Upon my head they placed a fruitless crown
> And put a barren scepter in my gripe.   (III.i.61–62)

If *King Lear* is a morality play in which Lear ultimately moves toward the good counselors Cordelia and Kent and away from the savage Goneril and Regan, *Macbeth* too is a morality play in which the tragic protagonist chooses the forces of evil rather than of good (Lady Macbeth and the witches rather than

Duncan and Banquo), but he is always aware of what he has done, and this self-awareness and the sense of guilt it engenders keep a hold on our goodwill and gain him some sympathy. He knows from the outset what is morally right and what is morally wrong; but because he does not know himself, he does not know that the means he takes to procure what he thinks is his good (the happiness attendant on kingship) will destroy his good. Our perception of his virtues, of his deep sufferings, and of his awareness of the ruin he has brought on himself prevent us from fully acquiescing in Malcolm's simple characterization of Macbeth as a "butcher" or from acquiescing in Jan Kott's recent reductive characterization of the play as one that reveals "the absurdity of the human situation."

Like *Macbeth*, *Antony and Cleopatra* has political implications, but it too is very different from Shakespeare's history plays. And it is very different from *Macbeth*, not only in its much wider geographical spread and in its diffusion of interest over two central figures, but in its conception of the tragic figure. There is no moral ambiguity about Macbeth; however we may view his early heroism and his continued sufferings from his conscience, we know—as he knows—that he is a murderer, not "an honorable murderer" (Othello's description of himself) but simply a murderer. Nothing extenuates his guilt. But in *Antony and Cleopatra* the case is not so clear, and it is not easy to decide whether the two lovers are, to put it simply, mostly good or mostly bad. Bernard Shaw, in the Preface to *Three Plays for Puritans*, summed it up thus: "After giving a faithful picture of the soldier broken down by debauchery, and the typical wanton in whose arms such men perish, Shakespeare finally strains all his huge command of rhetoric and stage pathos to give a theatrical sublimity to the wretched end of the business, and to persuade foolish spectators that the world was well lost by the twain." Certainly Shakespeare does not minimize Antony's debauchery or Cleopatra's wantonness. The first line of the play speaks of Antony's "dotage," and the speech goes on to contrast the present debauched Antony—a mere heavy-breathing sensualist—with the splendid Antony who was once a glorious military hero. Cleopatra is a

gypsy—that is, not merely an Egyptian but a lecherous trickster. Antony himself later says that Cleopatra "like a right
gypsy hath at fast and loose/Beguiled me" (IV.xii.28–29). It
is easy to find additional evidence for this view: Antony's
military wisdom disappears, and he is foolish enough to think
that Octavius Caesar may fight him in single combat (Enobarbus knows better, in III.xiii, when he says of this belief, "Caesar, thou hast subdued/His judgment too"); Antony foolishly
fights at sea, though he knows Caesar has the advantage there;
he lapses into hysterical sadism when he orders Thidias to be
whipped; and (to cut short what could be a long list) he
bungles his suicide.

But this is not the whole story. Although the Romans in
the play—and Antony himself, at times—judge the new Antony by the Roman standards of duty and military valor
and justly find a sad falling-off, the chief spokesman for Rome,
Caesar, is unattractive: he violates his treaty with Pompey,
he eradicates his partner Lepidus, he uses his sister Octavia
as a political pawn, and he seeks to deceive Cleopatra. It is no
accident that Shakespeare allows him no soliloquies; we see
Octavius only as a political man with no inner life. Moreover,
there is another way, a non-Roman way, of looking at Antony.
The new Antony, transformed by Cleopatra, can say,

> Let Rome in Tiber melt, and the wide arch
> Of the ranged empire fall! Here is my space,
> Kingdoms are clay: our dungy earth alike
> Feeds beast as man. The nobleness of life
> Is to do thus; when such a mutual pair
> And such a twain can do't.   (I.i.33–38)

In short the Roman code—especially as embodied in the cold,
triumphant Caesar—itself seems unattractive when compared
with some of the activities of Antony and Cleopatra. Caesar
sees Antony as a reveler engaged in "lascivious wassails" and
eating epicurean foods, and he contrasts him to the former
Antony, who on his campaigns ate "the roughest berry on the
rudest hedge" (I.iv.64). But Caesar's asceticism and hard-deal-
ing leave no room for warm friendships or even for the kind
of courteous sympathy that Antony can offer the simple Lep-

idus, the third but negligible triumvir. When Caesar invites Antony to visit Caesar's sister, with a view toward a political marriage, Antony says,

> Let us, Lepidus,
> Not lack your company.

And Lepidus warmly responds,

> Noble Antony,
> Not sickness should detain me.   (II.ii.170–71)

Later, Antony warns Lepidus that he is in danger:

> These quicksands, Lepidus,
> Keep off them, for you sink.   (II.vii.60–61)

Early in the play Lepidus himself gives us a vision of Antony that is an alternative to the narrow Roman view. To Caesar's assertion that Antony is "th' abstract of all faults/That all men follow" (that is, the symbol of universal weakness), Lepidus counters:

> I must not think there are
> Evils enow to darken all his goodness;
> His faults, in him, seem as the spots of heaven,
> More fiery by night's blackness, hereditary
> Rather than purchased [acquired], what he cannot change
> Than what he chooses.   (I.iv.10–15)

It is interesting to note that although Lepidus sees Antony's faults and describes them as darkness, he later reverses the dark-light symbolism and describes the "faults" as "the spots of heaven,/More fiery by night's blackness." Even Antony's faults, Lepidus argues, have a kind of heavenly luminosity, a shining virtue in them. For example, Antony is politically irresponsible and a sensualist, but these traits are not simply flaws in a basically good man; paradoxically, they are the qualities that help to make him glorious. (We will see something of the same paradox in Coriolanus.) Something along the same lines can be said of Cleopatra, and indeed Enobarbus says it. To Maecenas' statement that Antony must leave Cleopatra, Enobarbus replies:

> Never; he will not:
> Age cannot wither her, nor custom stale
> Her infinite variety: other women cloy
> The appetites they feed, but she makes hungry
> Where most she satisfies; for vilest things
> Become themselves [are becoming] in her, that the holy priests
> Bless her when she is riggish [wanton].   (II.ii.236–42)

This sort of ambiguity runs throughout the play. Even at the end, for example, Cleopatra's suicide has its noble aspect ("Husband, I come:/Now to that name my courage prove my title"), its sensuous aspect ("The stroke of death is as a lover's pinch,/Which hurts, and is desired"), and perhaps its cowardly aspect, for she knows that Caesar plans to humiliate her publicly, and thus her death is as much an escape from Caesar as a reunion with Antony. But it has its glory—the lines persuade us of that—and this glory is only dimmed, not dispelled, by Caesar's wry comment:

> Her physician tells me
> She hath pursued conclusions infinite
> Of easy ways to die.   (V.ii.353–55)

Despite such information, the final impression must be one of grandeur, evoking what Horatio in *Hamlet* calls "wonder." With a hero who is related to Hercules and described as a "grand sea," a man "past the size of dreaming," with a heroine who is "a lass unparalleled," and with a vast geographical sweep and abundant cosmic imagery, *Antony and Cleopatra* —for all of its evident sordidness—anticipates Shakespeare's last plays, the "romances," in which tragic woe yields to a sense of wonder attendant upon the revelation of a world in which love, forgiveness, and the imagination dissolve faults and take us beyond the world of time.

Like *Antony and Cleopatra*, *Coriolanus*, Shakespeare's last tragedy, is chiefly drawn from Plutarch, but the world it depicts is utterly different. In *Antony and Cleopatra* Shakespeare conveys the expansiveness of the late Roman Republic, partly by the setting in Egypt but more significantly by the imperial hero whose story transcends the political motif.

Coriolanus, however, depicts a much earlier and narrower
world, the days of the early Republic, and there is a continual
insistence on the abrasive class conflict between the plebeians
and the patricians. Coriolanus is a hero, but his heroism is
unattractive, for it is exclusively military; thus we tend to
judge him rather than feel for him. Despite the glorification
of Coriolanus in the first part of the play, we find it difficult
to be warmed by his virtue, and even Coriolanus' mother,
from whom he learned his valor, tells him he is "too absolute."
It is a valor that is inhuman (Coriolanus is compared to an
engine, and he compares himself to a dragon), a valor that is
an end in itself, unconnected with mankind, and finally an
enemy of mankind: "I will fight/Against my cank'red country
with the spleen/Of all the under fiends" (IV.v.94–96). It is this
valor, and not any sense of justice, that is almost the whole of
Coriolanus, as he tells us in the first act, when he conveys his
eagerness to fight against Tullus Aufidius, his only worthy
opponent:

> Were half to half the world by th' ears, and he
> Upon my party, I'd revolt, to make
> Only my wars with him. He is a lion
> That I am proud to hunt.   (I.i.235–38)

This sense of joyous energy is briefly catching, but in the end
Coriolanus remains unattractive, despite such tributes as "His
nature is too noble for the world" and "He shall have a noble
memory." Part of the trouble is his abundant railing, which
is never quite redeemed by a noble vision, for it is too rooted in
contempt of the lesser people around him. Coriolanus' rebuke
of the cowardly soldiers (I.iv.30–34), for instance, is perilously
close to the invective spewed by the misanthropic Thersites
in *Troilus and Cressida* or by Timon in the latter part of
Timon of Athens. Even when Coriolanus proudly rejects
Rome, "Thus I turn my back;/There is a world elsewhere"
(III.iii.135–36), we find that the world elsewhere is not a nobler
vision and a deeper awareness of self (as it is in the wise madness of Lear) but only Coriolanus' insistence that he will not
be other than himself. And he never perceives that what he is

is not everything that is worthwhile. The idea that each of Shakespeare's heroes suffers from a tragic "flaw" was briefly discussed and rejected earlier (see p. 141), but if the old idea that a tragic hero is characterized by *hybris* (overweening pride) truly applies to any of them it applies to Coriolanus. In IV.vii.35–48 Aufidius suggests that Coriolanus' fault may be "pride" or "defect of judgment." In the first act, before Coriolanus appears, two Citizens discuss him. The First Citizen says Coriolanus is "proud," to which the Second Citizen replies, "What he cannot help in his nature you account a vice in him." Perhaps it is not exactly "pride" that characterizes Coriolanus, for he is unwilling—indeed, in most of the play unable—to boast of his exploits. But this insistence on isolation, which is his nature, is almost the whole of him: "He is himself alone," "one thing," and this self or thing serves him wonderfully in war but incapacitates him in peace. When he puts off his valor there is nothing left of him:

> O my mother, mother! O!
> You have won a happy victory to Rome;
> But, for your son—believe it, O, believe it!—
> Most dangerously you have with him prevailed,
> If not most mortal to him.   (V.iii.185–89)

"Mercy" has drained his "honor," and Aufidius knows that he can at last defeat Coriolanus. Coriolanus regains his identity when, stung by Aufidius' rebuke, he reminds his Volscian enemies of his earlier conquest over them; yet this outburst of pride is what destroys him, for it stirs the Volscians to murder him. Thus although his heroism is never in doubt, Shakespeare's last tragic hero has less of the complex humanity of the earlier heroes. His code, which involves abundant contempt, not only keeps us at a distance; it also blinds him—though not us—to what is going on. He sees himself as his own master, but we see, ironically, that lesser people can manipulate him. (In the vulnerability and perhaps even inhumanity of his apartness Coriolanus bears some relation to Prospero in Shakespeare's last play, *The Tempest*. But Prospero learns fellow-feeling and is restored to his dukedom. But that is to move from the last tragedy to the last play, near in time, and related, but different: the tragic heroes cannot be restored to dukedoms.)

TWO SATIRIC TRAGEDIES:
TROILUS AND CRESSIDA, TIMON OF ATHENS

Probably the term "satiric" is a little too strong to describe these two plays, for they do not really hoot at their characters. Still, the characters are seen in such an ironic light and from such a detached point of view—even in comparison with *Coriolanus*—that "satiric tragedy" may be a useful starting place.

For the Renaissance, satire and tragedy were not far apart; satire was sometimes thought to have developed from tragedy. Here is John Milton's comment on the relationship: "A Satire, as it was born out of a Tragedy, so ought to resemble his parentage, to strike high, and adventure dangerously at the most eminent vices among the greatest persons." Although *Troilus and Cressida* and *Timon of Athens* are far apart in quality and can only be crudely linked together, "eminent vices" of great men in the ancient world are found in both of them. (Renaissance admiration of the classics did not always extend to Greek legendary figures. The Elizabethans held Virgil's *Aeneid*, which is unfriendly toward the Greeks, in too high esteem to see the Greeks as shining heroes.)

Troilus and Cressida, incomparably the better play, is probably the earlier of the two (1601–02 is the date usually given, that is, about the time of *Hamlet* and before *Othello, Lear,* and *Macbeth*). The difficulty of classifying it was apparent in its own day: the title page of the quarto calls it a history, the preface to the quarto says it is "comical," and the editors of the First Folio planned to put it with the tragedies, but they finally put it in unnamed territory between the histories and the tragedies, though they added the word "tragedy" to its title. This ambiguity has helped to make the play (rarely staged before the twentieth century) popular in our age, an age of Absurd drama, an age in which, Ionesco has said, the only possible reaction left is to "laugh at it all" because "everything has ceased to matter."

It is a very strange play; the preface's statement that it was "never staled with the stage, never clapper-clawed with the palms of the vulgar," leads us to think that it may have been written for a select audience rather than for the public theater, or that if it was written for the public theater it was found unsuitable. *Troilus* has two stories, one of politics and war concerning the Greeks who besiege Troy and who finally kill Hector, and another of love concerning Cressida's infidelity to Troilus. But despite the Prologue, which leads us to expect high military exploits, there is no heroic battle, and despite the lovers there is no joyous marriage; both stories deal with treachery and the destruction of merit by baseness. Moreover, much of the play is marked by disappointment, anticlimax, and frustration. For example, Hector argues that Helen should be returned to Menelaus, but then he withdraws his argument; Ulysses constructs an elaborate plot to get Achilles to fight, but when Achilles fights it is for a different reason; Pandarus' plot comes to nothing; Troilus is painfully disillusioned, but he does not press on to arrive at deep understanding, especially self-knowledge; and Thersites, a sort of heightened—or, better, lowered—version of the melancholy Jaques in *As You Like It* and of the carping Malvolio in *Twelfth Night,* regularly gives us a world of tragedy but also of satire. Ezra Pound said, we recall, that satire "draws one to consider time wasted." Tragedy too conveys a sense of waste, but in tragedy it is the result of nobility that is cut short, whereas in *Troilus* nobility is in very short supply.

Thersites, who sees only "Lechery, lechery, still wars and lechery" (V.ii.192–93), has a parallel in Pandarus, the commentator on the love story, but their low view of life is not the only one, and though the higher views come to nothing, their presence makes the play something other than a denunciation of mankind. The human beings are satirized, but the ideals—heroism and love—are not thereby debunked. Troilus has an air of the romantic lover of the comedies. If we recall

Bassanio's description in *The Merchant of Venice* of Portia as a treasure to be adventured for (I.i.161–76), we can see the resemblance in these lines of Troilus':

> Her bed is India; there she lies, a pearl.
> Between our Ilium and where she resides
> Let it be called the wild and wand'ring flood,
> Ourself the merchant, and this sailing Pandar
> Our doubtful hope, our convoy and our bark. (I.i.103–07)

Still, there is something more frenetic here, as there is in Troilus' apprehensiveness that love may be

> some joy too fine,
> Too subtle, potent, tuned too sharp in sweetness
> For the capacity of my ruder powers.
> I fear it much; and I do fear besides
> That I shall lose distinction [ability to distinguish] in my joys.
> (III.ii.21–25)

And none of the romantic heroes in the comedies is so sensual as to explain to his beloved that "the monstruosity in love" is "that the will is infinite and the execution confined; that the desire is boundless and the act a slave to limit" (III.ii.80–82). Troilus nevertheless is a lover, and Thersites' "lechery" is not quite apt. What sharply separates this play from the comedies is not the lover's attitude but the beloved's deeds: Cressida is false, and thus Troilus' love for her is put into an ironic light as Othello's (another warrior-lover) is not. Similarly, Hector, who had nobly refused to fight the disarmed Achilles, is himself slain by Achilles' henchmen when he is unarmed. It is not quite true, then, that (as Thersites says of the war) "all the argument is a whore and a cuckold," but it is true that the noble alternatives are powerless. The play contains Shakespeare's most famous speech on order (I.iii.78–136), but it is a dramatic representation of disorder.

  Timon of Athens has affinities with *Troilus and Cressida*, most notably in its images of disease (especially sexual) and in the railings of Apemantus, which resemble those of Thersites, and more pervasively in the ironic view we are invited to take. But it has affinities with both *Antony and Cleopatra* and *Coriolanus* (the three plays are indebted to Plutarch and probably were written within a few years of each other) in its concern with a hero who becomes an exile from society. This concern also relates *Timon* to *King Lear,* and it has been suggested that before Shakespeare thoroughly revised *Timon* he set to work on *King Lear* and then, having made what use he wanted to make of a man driven to distraction by ingratitude, he found no reason to return to *Timon.*

The chief problem is this: What are we to make of Timon's initial generosity and of his later misanthropy? Is the play the tragedy of a magnanimous man who is undone by his virtue —that is, by his high view of men, which men do not fulfill and which therefore drives him to misanthropy? Or is the play a satire of both his generosity and his misanthropy? In support of the first view, one can quote lines that praise Timon— lines that are not flattery because they are not spoken in his presence—such as the reference to "his good and gracious nature" (I.i.56) and the assertion that "The noblest mind he carries/That ever governed man" (I.i.289–90). His steward Flavius testifies on his behalf, at first in words but later in deeds when he seeks out his former master. Flavius, a follower of a fallen master, thus resembles Kent in *King Lear.* Late in the play Flavius sees Timon as a man

> brought low by his own heart,
> Undone by goodness. Strange, unusual blood,
> When man's worst sin is, he does too much good.
> Who then dares to be half so kind again?
> For bounty, that makes gods, do still mar men.   (IV.ii.37–41)

Against this high view of Timon it can be argued that two technicalities suggest that the play is not a tragedy (although the Folio puts it with the tragedies): first, though Timon is said to be "brought low by his own heart," his death, in fact, does not result from action (indeed, his death seems curiously irrelevant), and second, the Folio denies to *Timon* alone the word "tragedy" in the title, calling the play *The Life of Timon of Athens.* Moreover, even in the first scene Timon is not merely generous; he is also responsive to flattery, and his gifts are ostentatious and apparently a means of self-aggran-dizement. When he cannot bolster himself in this way, he falls into misanthropy, seeing mankind's faults but not his own. Here a comparison with Lear may be useful. Timon and Lear are both outcasts, and both rail against society, but Timon has little of interest to say about society and nothing of interest to say about himself, whereas Lear's denunciation of society—though mad—is touched with sympathy for those who suffer injustice and with an awareness of his own faults. Lear arrives at a vision larger than the one he first held; Timon merely exchanges an exalted view of man for a base one. Alcibiades puts it thus: "The middle of humanity thou never knewest, but the extremity of both ends" (IV.iii.299–300). This polarization, incidentally, relates *Timon* to Shakespeare's last plays, the romances, in which characters tend to be either good or bad rather than "of a mingled yarn, good and ill together." And, more to our purpose here, it relates *Timon* to the other tragedies—*Macbeth, Antony and Cleopatra, Coriolanus*—that follow *King Lear,* forming a group of plays whose heroes finally seem (as Lear does not) deficient in moral value. The heroes of the earlier great tragedies are no less extreme in their unwillingness to accept the way of the world; that is why they are heroes. But they also know the middle of humanity, and they embody a value that seems to enrich the world around them; that is why we feel their sufferings as our own, and we treasure their experiences. In any case, *Timon* is a failure, and one is inclined to think that Shakespeare, who so often and so consummately calls our attention to the power of generosity, found misanthropy too repellent a theme to engage his powers fully.

10

The Nondramatic Works

Shakespeare's first work to appear in print was not a play but a narrative poem. Because the status of poet was higher than that of playwright in Elizabethan times—professional poets were dependent on courtly patronage, whereas most playwrights were dependent on the pennies of the general public —it. is likely that Shakespeare thought, at least for a while, that his poetry rather than his plays would bring him lasting fame. This hypothesis receives some support from the fact that his two long narrative poems were published in remarkably accurate texts, with dedications by the author. Shakespeare thus apparently had a hand in the publication of these poems, but he never concerned himself with the publication of the plays, and he wrote no further dedications.

Leisure time to write the two narratives was probably afforded by the plague, which closed the London theaters from the summer of 1592 to the spring of 1594. Shakespeare's first published work, *Venus and Adonis* (1593), is an artful, erotic poem of 1194 lines that was calculated to please a noble patron, the youthful Earl of Southampton, whose taste presumably had been developed by ornate and erotic mythological pieces such as Lodge's *Scylla's Metamorphosis* (1589). Marlowe's *Hero and Leander* (1593 or earlier, although not published until 1598) belongs to the same school of serious yet predominantly witty and decorative poetry. *Venus and Adonis* has been much praised for its realistic passages about horses, birds, the doe, and especially the hare (lines 679–708); but however we may value these passages, which seem derived from Warwickshire

memories, the poem as a whole produces the effect not of realism but of most cunning artifice. It is less a photograph than
a tapestry, less a description of creatures moving in external
nature than a presentation of abstract types set in a hothouse;
or we can vary the figure and see the poem as Hazlitt did,
when, calling attention to the frigidity of this poem about passion, he characterized it as an icehouse. Attempts to salvage it
by finding in it anticipations of Shakespeare's later plays (a
background of love in the woods, *A Midsummer Night's
Dream* and *As You Like It*; a self-centered young man, *All's
Well*; a destructive beauty, *Antony and Cleopatra*) do not
quite succeed. But *Venus and Adonis* apparently worked for
its contemporary readers: there were at least ten editions of
the poem in Shakespeare's lifetime; a contemporary writer
noted that "the younger sort takes much delight in Shakespeare's *Venus and Adonis*"; and in a satiric play of 1601, a
foolish courtier refers to the poem, saying, "I'll worship sweet
master Shakespeare, and to honor him will lay his *Venus and
Adonis* under my pillow."

In 1594 Shakespeare followed this bid for noble patronage
with the publication of a second poem (the "graver labour" he
had promised in the dedication to *Venus*) dedicated to Southampton, *The Rape of Lucrece* (thus goes the running head;
the title page simply calls the poem *Lucrece*). Like *Venus and
Adonis*, it draws its central narrative from Ovid. In its depiction of Tarquin, who, overcome by passion, sacrifices honor
and gains only self-loathing and enmity, Shakespeare touches
on a tragic theme, and indeed in *Macbeth* he was later to mention Tarquin. Here is the passage from *Macbeth*, followed by
a passage from *Lucrece*:

> Now o'er the one half-world
> Nature seems dead, and wicked dreams abuse
> The curtained sleep; witchcraft celebrates
> Pale Hecate's offerings; and withered murder,
> Alarumed by his sentinel, the wolf,
> Whose howl's his watch, thus with his stealthy pace,
> With Tarquin's ravishing strides, towards his design
> Moves like a ghost.   (*Macbeth*, II.i.49–56)

Now stole upon the time the dead of night,
When heavy sleep had closed up mortal eyes.
No comfortable star did lend his light,
No noise but owls, and wolves' death-boding cries;
Now serves the season that they may surprise
    The silly lambs: pure thoughts are dead and still,
    While lust and murder wakes to stain and kill.

(Lucrece, lines 162–68)

In Lucrece's lamentations, and especially in Tarquin's internal debates, the universal stuff of tragedy is set forth in a narrative form, yet the final effect is far from tragic, for like *Venus and Adonis* the poem is so obviously ornate, so richly heraldic, so formal in its contrasts, that the manner overcomes the matter. It is a web of decorative (and sometimes very beautiful) passages; it is longer than *Venus and Adonis* (and fourteen times as long as its source), but the greater length is due not to additional action but to even greater elaboration of the little there is.

Among the nondramatic poems the sonnets have won widespread praise. They belong to a genre made famous in Italy by Petrarch (1304–74); Petrarch was imitated in England by Wyatt and by Surrey, some of whose poems were published in 1557 in a book that is usually called *Tottel's Miscellany.* But sonneteering did not become a national pastime in England until 1591, when the posthumous publication of Sir Philip Sidney's *Astrophel and Stella* started the vogue. The Italian or Petrarchan sonnet is basically a two-part poem, consisting of an octave rhyming *abbaabba* and a sestet, normally in a somewhat different tone of voice, rhyming *cdecde* or *cdcdcd,* or another variant. The English sonnet (sometimes called Shakespearean, though Shakespeare did not invent the form) is a four-part poem, consisting of three quatrains and a couplet: *abab cdcd efef gg.* The couplet normally provides a syntactically independent aphoristic summary. But the thought of the sonnet does not always follow the rhyme scheme, that is, it does not always break after each quatrain. In a good number of Shakespeare's sonnets the chief turn comes, as in an Italian sonnet, after the eighth line.

Shakespeare's *Sonnets* was not published until 1609, but surely most and possibly all of the 154 sonnets that make up the book had been written at least a decade earlier. The exact date of composition is unknown, but the early and middle nineties seems reasonable for most of them. (There are also sonnets in *Love's Labor's Lost* and *Romeo and Juliet,* plays of the middle nineties.) In 1598 Francis Meres alluded to Shakespeare's "sugared sonnets." "Sugared" is appropriate for at least some of them: there are poems that show a delight in ingenious conceits of the kind we associate with the earlier plays. But other sonnets are masterful in their apparent simplicity of utterance that, coupled with a depth of view, makes the poems among the world's greatest. If the best sonnets were written before 1598 (rather than shortly before publication in 1609), Shakespeare achieved maturity in the sonnet more quickly than in the drama. The 154 poems do not narrate a continuous story, but there are groups of related sonnets; for example, Sonnets 1–17 are all written to an aristocratic young man, urging him to marry. Although the *Sonnets* may be indebted to some contact that Shakespeare had with members of the aristocracy, they cannot be read as sheer autobiography (though of course they often ring true). The usual motifs of Elizabethan sonnets can be found—the poet eternizes his patron; the eye and the heart are at war—but there is also a new range of feeling that has affinities with *Lucrece* and therefore approaches a tragic view. For instance, in *Lucrece* Shakespeare gives us this insight into one kind of tragic experience:

> Those that much covet are with gain so fond
> That what they have not, that which they possess
> They scatter and unloose it from their bond,
> And so by hoping more they have but less;
> Or, gaining more, the profit of excess
>   Is but to surfeit, and such griefs sustain
>   That they prove bankrout in this poor rich gain.
>
> (lines 134–40)

After he rapes Lucrece, Tarquin is compared to a "full-fed hound or gorgèd hawk," now loathing what he had before pursued:

> His taste delicious, in digestion souring,
>   Devours his will, that lived by foul devouring.   (lines 699–700)

Every poem is complete in itself and ought not to be reduced or expanded to coincide with any other poem, but we can see in these passages from *Lucrece* something akin to Sonnet 129, a passionate analysis of lust before, during, and after consummation.

> Th' expense of spirit* in a waste of shame
> Is lust in action; and, till action, lust
> Is perjured, murd'rous, bloody, full of blame,
> Savage, extreme, rude, cruel, not to trust;
> Enjoyed no sooner but despisèd straight;
> Past reason hunted, and no sooner had,
> Past reason hated as a swallowed bait
> On purpose laid to make the taker mad;
> Made† in pursuit, and in possession so;
> Had, having, and in quest to have, extreme;
> A bliss in proof, and proved, a very woe,
> Before, a joy proposed; behind, a dream.
>   All this the world well knows, yet none knows well
>   To shun the heaven that leads men to this hell.

Not all Shakespeare's sonnets, of course, are like this, and our interest in the tragedies ought not to lead us to concentrate on poems about lust or the destructive will to the exclusion of, say, those celebrations of beauty that are equally impressive. In short, the sonnets are remarkably varied—disordered, as some readers who cherish a consistent story would say. There is a young aristocrat and a dark lady (who was the poet's mistress and who also has had an affair with the young man), both of whom evoke varying degrees of admiration and distress from the speaker of the sonnets. If we look for a dominant subject, we perhaps find it in Time. Time is a destroyer, as in Sonnet 65:

> Since brass, nor stone, nor earth, nor boundless sea,
>   But sad mortality o'ersways their power,

---

* "Th' expense of spirit" is the expenditure of vital power, and more specifically, perhaps, of semen.
† "Made" is often emended to "mad," but can be taken as equivalent to "Made mad."

How with this rage shall beauty hold a plea,
Whose action is no stronger than a flower?   (lines 1–4)

But Time also engenders anew; and the poet's words re-create his subject, conferring on beauty a new existence that may arrest or at least seem to arrest the triumph of Time. If this inadequate description has any truth in it, the world of the sonnets is very near to that of the great plays.

The sonnets have been long esteemed, but a short poem called *The Phoenix and the Turtle* (1601) has only relatively recently gained universal praise, probably because in the 1920's admirers of John Donne and the other metaphysical poets helped to educate subsequent taste to appreciate this incantational, funereal poem about the transcendence of human love, conveyed through the symbols of the phoenix, a legendary bird that resurrects itself from its own ashes, and the turtledove, an emblem of constancy in love. *Venus and Adonis* can be coupled with *Lucrece,* and each sonnet can be coupled with the remaining 153, but *The Phoenix and the Turtle* stands alone. Yet in its faith in the power of a love that transcends reason, a love in which individuals are mysteriously joined and yet, equally mysteriously, retain their identity, it earns its place in a story that includes the sonnets, *Romeo and Juliet,* and *Antony and Cleopatra.*

Part Three

MODERN PRODUCTIONS

11

A Note on Staging Shakespeare

It is evident that a production of a play can reveal meanings that a reader may miss. However proud a reader may be of the theater under his hat, he knows that an intelligently directed and skillfully acted performance has a power that he cannot equal alone. One understands what a reviewer meant when, decades ago, he said of Edith Evans' Rosalind in *As You Like It,* "She made the audience one Orlando." But the advantage is not always on the side of production. For example, reacting against traditions of grand and mellifluous speaking, actors who attempt to portray character realistically sometimes obliterate the poetry by inappropriate emphases and pauses. Such a constriction of Shakespeare is only one symptom of the difficulty that faces every conscientious director.

The difficulty, of course, is that the director must decide how this word should be uttered, what gestures should accompany that speech, how this actor should exit, and so on. Understandably, he sometimes finds he can avoid innumerable local decisions by imposing on the play a single grand idea. But to make this idea come across, the play must be cut and scenes transposed. These changes are then justified by appealing to Elizabethan theater-practice and by raising the bogy of "museum-theater," connoting a faithful and (it is implied) therefore lifeless production. (Since we know almost nothing about the original presentations of Shakespeare, there is, in fact, no danger that directors will inflict on successive generations mere repetitions of what Shakespeare's audience saw. Museum-theater, when we talk of Shakespeare, can only mean the presentation of an unaltered text—scarcely a frightening procedure except for a few very long plays. And what is wrong with museum-theater in this sense? Every age, of course, will see the plays somewhat differently, but the plays themselves are what we should see, just as in an art museum we see the original, vital works, and we have protective glass and laws to keep people from adding mustaches and beards to make the paintings "relevant.")

One modern tendency in staging Shakespeare, perhaps originating from the idea that today's audience cannot possibly follow the words, emphasizes visual business, adding mimed prologues, tableaux effects, ritualistic dances, and spares no expense in its effort to enlighten the public. Such productions also do not hesitate to slow the play down, to cut lines in order to make up the time, and to prettify into a musical comedy a play that is secretly felt to be something of an embarrassment.

Curiously, the opposite tendency, bleak presentation of the plays on a bare stage, often reveals a similar distrust of the play, but now the play is assimilated not to musical comedy but to drama of the Absurd. Again lines and scenes are cut in order to gain time for huge silences, though these silences are intended to diminish the characters, whereas the rococo interpolations are intended to elevate them. Absurd Shakespeare is of course part of an attempt to make Shakespeare relevant. Speaking broadly, these productions tend toward debunking, toward cynicism, toward disbelief in heroism, in honor, in love, in happiness. So heroes are braggarts or hypocrites, those honored are senile or effeminate, lovers are lustful or idiotic. Now, as previous pages discussing each of Shakespeare's plays tried to show, Shakespeare was fully aware that heroism has its limits, that love has its folly, that human beings are not gods, but he seemed not to have felt that mankind therefore is contemptible or even that it is merely pitiful. Yet many productions remove the grandeur from the tragedies and the joy from the comedies. For example, it is rare to see a production of *The Merchant of Venice*—a play whose text ends with a bawdy joke—that does not end by giving Antonio a slow, solitary, melancholy exit.

The desire to be relevant often takes the naive form of using modern dress. Modern clothing is as good as earlier clothing (zippers are a good deal better than lacing), but it is sometimes at odds with the text. More important, many productions use it not simply to be contemporary but to make a point that is not really in the play. The most famous example is Orson Welles' production of *Julius Caesar* (1937), in which black shirts, along with fascist salutes, were used to turn the play from a tragedy into antifascist propaganda. In recent years, *Henry V, Troilus, Julius Caesar,* have been used to stir indignation against the war in Vietnam. So, too, *The Tempest* becomes only a play about colonialism, *Othello* about racism, and *Lear* about Samuel Beckett. The director, that is, is not staging the play but is using it as a vehicle for something else. And though the message may be worthy and relevant, the play suffers and hence we suffer. The play suffers because it is chopped or twisted into something it is not; we suffer because we are deprived of experiencing the play in all its fullness, all its irrelevance. Shakespeare's world in many ways is different from ours, and the best way for us to profit from Shakespeare is to be exposed to his world, with all its oddities, as fully as possible. In productions that trust Shakespeare's text, we may find some things that are dull or irrelevant or puzzling and some that accord with our world. We may also find in these humble productions some things that we wish to recover and bring into our in-some-ways impoverished world.

12

The Film Versions of Shakespeare

It comes as a surprise to learn from Robert Hamilton Ball's book *Shakespeare on Silent Film* that during the silent-movie era about four hundred films were derived from Shakespeare's plays. The earliest seems to have been made in 1899, only four years after movies were first shown as a popular entertainment. These early films, often only a few minutes long, were sometimes attempts to record permanently a famous actor's gestures in a famous scene; but probably the chief motive was a desire to demonstrate that movies were not mere novelties and could be "respectable."

A silent production of Shakespeare seems paradoxical, and yet when one studies the plays, one is impressed with how often costumes and gestures (see pp. 41–42) communicate important meanings. Shakespeare knew how to use all of the resources of a dramatist; it is also probably true that if one knows the gist of a plot, one can get something of the drama of a play even without hearing the dialogue. Anyone who has seen a play in a language that he does not understand knows that some of the meaning is communicated anyway, and if he has some previous familiarity with the play, he can follow the foreign (for him, in a sense, wordless) version pretty well.

Early film practice and theory naturally looked to Shakespeare because of the close connection between film and theater: although the earliest movies showed real-life happenings (workers leaving a factory, a train coming into a station), they very soon began to tell stories, and they easily assumed that a story acted before a camera is like a story acted before a spectator in the theater. Although film theoreticians realized relatively soon that film and theater are different media, they nevertheless still wished to attach to film some of the prestige of the theater, and Shakespeare seemed to provide abundant support. First, he was a popular artist, proof that an art designed for a mass audience could also be of high quality. Second, the conventions of the soliloquy and the aside were seen as anticipations of the film's close-up, with the character drawing an audience's attention away from the stage as a whole and exclusively to himself. Moreover, it was argued that because the Elizabethan playhouse was more compact than the large, modern playhouse, film close-ups could give the audience a better sense of what Elizabethans actually saw. Third, when the camera, no longer fixed in one position, began to move, giving close-up and panoramic shots, and when cutting and editing provided shots of different locations in quick succession, Shakespeare's quick and abundant changes of place (something like forty-two scenes in *Antony and Cleopatra*) were felt to be "cinematic," the play's locale changing as quickly and easily as in a film. (This notion persists. A contemporary critic, John F. Danby, says, "To describe the swiftness of *Antony and Cleopatra* we need to draw on the imagery of the cinema. There is more cinematic movement, more panning, tracking, and playing with the camera, more mixing of shots than in any other of Shakespeare's tragedies.")

Still, any attempt to assimilate Shakespeare's plays to film must necessarily recognize that this involves a transposition of a work from one medium into another. The question can be raised, Why transpose? (We can dismiss such nonsense as the remarks of George Schaeffer, producer of a filmed *Macbeth* in 1961: "Shakespeare was the first film scenarist. On film we are better able to do justice to his genius than on the stage. With a cinema screen as our canvas we are able to paint wider, brighter pictures, produce truer portraits of his characters, set them against the authentic backgrounds of which he could only dream.") After all, no one would turn *Hamlet* into a novel or *Macbeth* into a narrative poem. Yet, interestingly, there is, aside from film, one form into which Shakespeare's plays have fairly often and successfully been transposed, and that is opera. Like film, opera is highly visual; to put it a little differently, like film, opera does not much value words, for the words are often foreign to the audience or, if understood, rarely intelligible when they are sung. Perhaps we accept, indeed we value, Shakespeare in opera because we fully sense that the opera is largely independent of what we value most in Shakespeare's words; it is not offered to us as a substitute for the play. Opera is plot and character and music (words that are *sung*), not plot and character and words. (Significantly, perhaps the best operas derived from Shakespeare, Verdi's *Falstaff* and *Otello,* with librettos by Boito, are by men who could not read English.)

If opera offers plot and character and music, does a film of Shakespeare offer—in addition to plot and character—a balance of words and pictures? Probably not, partly because most spectators are not really very sensitive to pictures, and mostly because the words in a film—since they are not rendered unintelligible by music—insist on being heard. If we cannot hear the words clearly, as in Orson Welles' film of *Macbeth,* where a Scots accent and unfortunate recording practices distort them, we are annoyed. Moreover, when a critic praising Franco Zeffirelli's *Romeo and Juliet* (1968) assures us that the director did well to delete Juliet's famous speech beginning "Gallop apace, you fiery-footed steeds" because he achieved a cinematic analogy to her impatience by cutting rapidly from one shot to another, we may demur, preferring the lines to an analogy. Perhaps it is an unfortunate habit, but we go to the movie theater not only to see Shakespeare but to hear him; we treasure the words, and we are not prepared to accept pictures as generous compensation for deleted words. Of course we can delight in the pictures if they do not displace words. Max Reinhardt's *Midsummer Night's Dream* (1935) employed an interesting visual device to help interpret (but not to replace) the words of the fairies: he shot Oberon through a spangled gauze, giving an appropriately eerie effect to the words spoken by this ruler who is a "King of Shadows." But to the Shakespeare purist the least objectionable visual effects are those

that occur when lines are not being spoken: in the opening of
Grigori Kozintsev's *Hamlet* (1964), we first see the coastline,
then the castle, then riders (one of the riders proves to be
Hamlet) galloping toward the castle. Hamlet enters, the draw-
bridge rises, the portcullis descends, and thus we *see* that
"Denmark's a prison"; the pictures have not been at war with
the words nor (equally bad) have they been redundant; they
have served only as an interpretation of later words.

To what extent do we welcome pictures as a substitute for,
or supplement to, Shakespeare's words? Rudolf Arnheim's
maxim was that "sound film . . . is not a verbal masterpiece
supplemented by pictures, but a homogeneous creation of
word and picture which cannot be split up into parts that
have any meaning separately." But, of course, the problem is
precisely that in filming Shakespeare one *is* dealing with "a
verbal masterpiece." Roughly speaking, the less successful the
words—that is, the play—the more acceptable a substitution
of pictures is; so, for example, Zeffirelli's *Taming of the Shrew*
(1966) is a pleasant enough piece. Because most of us do not
supremely value the play, we are not disturbed by Zeffirelli's
diminution of the Lucentio-Bianca plot or by his spectacular
presentation of the wedding between Petruchio and Kate, a
scene Shakespeare did not show. But with plays that we value
highly, especially with their long speeches and, most especially, with those speeches that reveal subtle internal actions
(developments within the minds of the characters, rather than
external happenings), what sort of pictorial comment is acceptable and indeed meaningful? What are we to *see* when
we hear these speeches? (Laurence Olivier found he had to cut
Hamlet's soliloquy beginning "How all occasions do inform
against me" because "it proved intractable as cinematic material.") Putting aside long-shots that more or less give us a
tableau effect (used effectively in Olivier's *Henry V* and in
Akira Kurosawa's version of *Macbeth, Throne of Blood*), the
choice comes down to (1) middle-shots or close-ups of the
speaker; (2) reaction shots, in close-up, of auditors, and (3)
shots of images that correspond to the narrative or descriptive
content of the speech, if it has such content.

Close-ups of the speaker seem to be the favorite solution, but, as Olivier has said, this common cinematic way of getting emphasis often is at odds with the speeches, which build to "big" climaxes. Moreover, close-ups are often bothersome; we do not always want those moving or unmoving eyes, that wrinkled or smooth brow, that jawing mouth, to be so prominent, to be an equal partner with what is being said. The spectator at a performance of the play, fortunately, is at a decent distance from the actors, but the movie close-up brings us into such proximity that the image is able to overpower the words. (In *Romeo and Juliet,* Zeffirelli used lots of close-ups, but his solution to the problem of the relation of words to images was somewhat too simple: he drastically cut Romeo's and Juliet's speeches, leaving them to communicate mostly by smiles, sighs, and soulful looks.)

Reaction shots—let us say of Goneril while Lear is cursing her—do not always work either. Such shots rarely are appropriate for the big speeches of major characters because they seem to imply that the speaker's words are less important than the response to them, whereas the words often are most important for the speaker's own response to them, for the speaker's own mental development. When a minor character is speaking to a major character, however, reaction shots may be effective, as when the Nurse advises Juliet to forget Romeo, and we focus on Juliet's surprise, dismay, and evident rejection of this advice.

Finally, shots that correspond to the narrative content of the speech—the visual presentation in Olivier's *Hamlet* of Ophelia's body floating in the stream when the queen tells of Ophelia's drowning—are really suitable only for the relatively few speeches that have lots of narrative content. The device is offensively clever when, for example, in Peter Brook's *King Lear,* Gloucester's speech "As flies to wanton boys are we to the gods" is spoken in a long-shot, so that Gloucester and Edgar seem flylike in the otherwise empty space. Unless one already knows the play well, how does one know who is speaking the lines?

If these assumptions and conclusions are right, filmed Shakespeare is diminished Shakespeare except when the film is of a particularly thin play or, as we shall see, when the film quite deliberately uses Shakespeare only as a point of departure.

It is time to look at a few of the best-known films of Shakespeare. These can be arranged by type: (1) films of stage productions (Laurence Olivier's *Othello*); (2) films that depart from the conditions of the playhouse but seek to be fairly faithful to the text (Olivier's *Henry V*, his *Hamlet*, and Peter Brook's *King Lear*); (3) films that take Shakespeare as a point of departure (Orson Welles' *Chimes at Midnight*—retitled *Falstaff*—and Akira Kurosawa's *Throne of Blood*, derived from *Macbeth*).

Olivier's *Othello* (1965) seeks to give the viewer a sense of the play as he might see it in the theater. This humble aim is anathema to the cinéaste, who insists that cinema, when it is art, is an independent medium rather than a medium that records a stage performance. The usual claims are that cinema is primarily visual, the theater primarily aural; cinema is fluid, the theater tends to be static, confined to one or at most a few locales. And so in adapting a play to a film, it is usual to "open it up," extending the sense of space far beyond the few sets that a stage production can use. Olivier's film, then, violates some basic assumptions of film theory, but it is remarkably successful.

Othello was shot in a studio in which theater sets were constructed. Three wide-screen Panavision cameras recorded the long speeches simultaneously and then the shots were edited. Because the film seeks to reproduce fairly closely a performance in the theater, there is no background music and there are no exterior shots, though backlighting occasionally gives the effect of sea or sky, and the cameras are not confined, like a spectator in a theater, to a single position. On the whole the cameras are fairly close to the actors, but occasionally we get a tableau effect, and at least once—when Othello faints—we see the action from above the stage.

Given its aim—not at all despicable or trivial—the film is extremely effective. The virtues and faults are not cinematic but are those of the stage production. Olivier's interpretation perhaps overemphasizes Othello's primitiveness: he walks— often barefoot—with a rolling gait, and on the whole he conveys the director's unfortunate idea that "Othello is a pompous, word-spinning, arrogant black general." One can regret, too, the deletion of the play's opening scenes in Venice, but, again, these complaints may be equally lodged against the stage production on which the film was based. In short, in this film Olivier neatly demonstrates that a stage production, when transferred to the screen without much change, *can* provide an interesting evening. Give it A—, the minus not because it fails to be truly cinematic but because the conception of the protagonist is not fully satisfactory.

Twenty-one years earlier, in *Henry V* (1944), Olivier had been freer. The film of *Henry V* follows an abridged text of the play very closely, but it is a photographed stage play only near the beginning and at the end, when we see what is supposed to be an Elizabethan production in Shakespeare's Globe Theatre. Encompassed within this frame, the central portion of the film makes considerable use of painted backdrops, not in an effort to reproduce a stage production but in an effort to evoke the medieval illuminations of the age of Henry V. It is all very pretty and in keeping with Olivier's presentation of Henry as a charming young man. One of the most memorable scenes, however, the battle of Agincourt, was filmed out-of-doors. Though ever since Eisenstein's *Alexander Nevsky,* battle scenes are always pretty much the same, with the camera tracking along, looking down a line of advancing horsemen, one can scarcely imagine a better treatment of this scene, which, of course, does not occur on stage in the play. Theoretically, the two styles—picturesque sets and realistic locations—ought to produce dissonance, but each is so pleasant in itself that it would be carping to demand consistency. Finally, it should be mentioned that the film was made when England was preparing to invade German-occupied France, and so the militarism that Henry engagingly preaches is understandably presented without any of the criticism of it that Shakespeare built into the play. Henry's order to cut the throats of the

French prisoners is deleted from the film, lest the barbarism cast doubt on the nobility of conquest, and on the whole the battle is graceful rather than gory. Give the film an A, not as innovative cinema but as the first Shakespearean film to maintain a consistently high level of excellence (Reinhardt's *Midsummer Night's Dream* [1935] and George Cukor's *Romeo and Juliet* [1936], with Norma Shearer and Leslie Howard, are much more uneven). The film has now been transferred to SuperScope, which deletes about one-third of the image from the top and bottom of the screen, so there are now funny shots of Olivier from mid-thigh to eyebrows. Even so, and with a sound track much damaged by splicing, *Henry V* remains a delight.

Olivier's *Hamlet* (1948) is much less successful, partly because no version (on the stage or in the movie theater) can ever fully satisfy, but chiefly because Olivier adopts a philistine interpretation of Hamlet. At the beginning of the film we are informed that the play is the tragedy of a man who could not make up his mind, and this crude interpretation dominates not only Olivier's conception of the character but, naturally, his way of filming the whole story. Take the sets: Olivier told the designer, Roger Furse, that he wanted the castle to be "a dream-like, cavernous place," appropriate for the "shadowy regions of the hero's mind." And take the camera work: deep-focus photography that allows both the background and the foreground to be in sharp focus and permits unusually prolonged shots of characters walking here and there, with the camera often ascending, descending, and circling to give us a continual sense of uncertainty. Luckily, this sense of uncertainty goes beyond the announced conception of an irresolute Hamlet and sometimes gets us near to the heart of the play: the difficulty of acting in a world of uncertainties and in a world where action seems useless. (As Erwin Panofsky suggests in an essay on film, cinema is an art that conveys emotion by the shifting of spaces, light, and shadow, most notably in chase scenes. Olivier's *Hamlet* is largely a psychological chase presented in spatial images.) Doubtless the camera is kept in motion also because Olivier fears the spectators might otherwise grow bored, but it seems clear that the primary reason is an effort to interpret the play in cinematic terms.

Olivier consistently tries also to communicate through visual images of place. Roger Furse has said that the "topmost tower of the battlements . . . might almost be given a credit among the actors. It is the first thing to be seen when the film opens, and it reinforces the dramatic effect on several occasions. It is to this lonely height that Hamlet is led by the Ghost"; later Hamlet meditates on suicide from this dangerous height; finally, his corpse is carried to it, thus suggesting that the tragic hero—almost by definition a figure associated with lonely heights—has finally achieved peace in his apartness.

Finally, a few words about the modernizations and the cuts in the text of this *Hamlet*. The modernizations are harmless: "wandering and uneasy spirit" instead of Shakespeare's "extravagant and erring spirit," "roar" instead of "bruit," and so on. The cuts are more bothersome, but the four and a half hours of the play had to be somehow reduced to about two and a half hours. Olivier tried to cover himself, saying that the film should be regarded as an "Essay in *Hamlet*," a kind of creative sketch, and "not as a film version of a necessarily abridged classic." Rosencrantz and Guildenstern are deleted (big deletions were necessary) and so is Fortinbras. Also deleted are two soliloquies ("O what a rogue and peasant slave am I" and "How all occasions do inform against me") and innumerable parts of scenes. Despite heavy deletions, however, the film remains too close to the play to be considered without reference to the play, and such reference works to the film's disadvantage. Give it B.

Like Olivier's *Hamlet*, Peter Brook's *King Lear* (1971) departs from the conditions of the playhouse and yet it too (despite heavy cuts) remains uncomfortably close to the play, seeming to mangle rather than to transpose it. Something like four hours of playing time are reduced to two hours and fifteen minutes, many of the cuts being made to emphasize—or to manufacture—a kinship between *King Lear* and Absurdist drama. And so *King Lear* is turned into a mean thing. For example, Brook deletes Lear's initial ceremonious entrance at the head of a procession of dukes, princesses, and attendants; when we first see him in the film, he is already seated, a zombie in a barren land rather than a potent figure presiding over a kingdom "with shadowy forests and with champains riched,/ With plenteous rivers and wide-skirted meads." Near the end of the film, Edgar's ceremonious challenge to Edmund is deleted in a final effort to strip the play of whatever splendor it has. (Why do film-makers—except when filming *Romeo and Juliet*—turn a deaf ear to John Milton's apt description of "*gorgeous* tragedy"? Why, too, does Brook deprive Cordelia of her touching love for Lear? Because Brook wants to reduce the tragic to the grotesque.) The cuts and the transpositions of speeches are so substantial that much of the film is unintelligible to a viewer who does not have Shakespeare's text in mind, and this is not an accident or a miscalculation: the play has deliberately been rendered meaningless because that is what Brook wants it to be. Utterly puzzling yet representative shots are those introducing Edmund and Edgar, where one often cannot tell which of these two opposed characters is speaking, and the scene of Goneril's death, where she mysteriously writhes about and dashes her head against a rock. Sometimes voices are heard but the speakers cannot be identified (as in Absurdist drama, words are not a means of communicating but of revealing the impossibility of communicating); often the camera gives us the lower half of the face or the back of a head. (In Jean-Luc Godard's *Vivre Sa Vie* most of the first scene, after the credits, also shows us the backs of the characters, but Godard gives us these relatively unexpressive images in order to force us to concentrate on what is being said, whereas Brook gives them in deliberate, and successful, but meaningless efforts to create alienation.) At one point there is what seems like a steal from Ingmar Bergman's *Persona*, a pretense of projector breakdown. There are some good things in the film, notably toward the end when Lear and the blind Gloucester meet, but as a whole it is a pretentious and ugly diminution of the play. Give it C—.

Moving from films that more or less try to present a cinematic version of a play to films that are free reworkings of a
play or plays, one inevitably thinks of Orson Welles' *Falstaff*
(1966) and of Akira Kurosawa's *Throne of Blood* (1957). *Falstaff*, a ninety-two minute film, is chiefly drawn from *1 and 2
Henry IV*, but it also is indebted to *Richard II, Henry V*, and
The Merry Wives of Windsor. Welles characterized his film as
"a dark comedy, the story of the betrayal of a friendship" and
as a depiction of "the death of Merrie England." Something of
this is implicit in the original title, *Chimes at Midnight*,
drawn from one of Falstaff's lines when, with the ancient Justice Shallow, he reminisces about his lusty youth: "We have
heard the chimes at midnight, Master Shallow." No one would
say that the plays of *Henry IV* can be adequately characterized
thus, but by drawing upon so much material and by converting
it into a film that is shorter than any one of the plays, Welles
effectively prevents a close comparison with Shakespeare; we
accept his statement (as we do not accept Olivier's about *Hamlet*) that *Falstaff* is "really quite a different drama."

There is a lot wrong with *Falstaff*, but most of the faults are
mechanical matters of a fairly minor order. Plagued by financial problems, Welles had to adopt drastic solutions. For example, since some of the major actors were not available when
he was shooting certain scenes, he used long-shots, substituting doubles; uneasy at working with English actors whom
he could get for only short periods, he recorded his own
dialogue separately, and the imperfect synchronization shows.

Still, the film is a triumph: Shakespeare's words have been
edited into a meaningful new scenario that is superbly acted
and shot. The visual images genuinely help to bring out the
meaning of the play: there are beautiful rapid tracking shots
of the exuberant robbery in the woods, there are beautiful
shots by a hand-held camera of Falstaff bustling in the busy
tavern, and there are beautiful low-angle shots emphasizing
Falstaff's bulk, the icy King Henry IV in his appropriately cold,
lofty castle, and Hal's powerful rejection of Falstaff at last.
But it is in the battle scene that the camera does its best work,
perhaps because the actors' faces are masked by helmets and

because the scene is wordless. Probably the influence of Eisenstein can be felt in the anonymity of the mass of combatants, the wordlessness, the emphasis on the expanse of mud of the battlefield (compare the sea in *Potemkin*), and the rapid cutting, but the best description of the scene is Welles': "What I was planning to do—and did—was to intercut the shots in which the action was contrary, so that every cut seemed to be a blow, a counter-blow, a blow received, a blow returned." Give it A.

Probably the only film derived from Shakespeare that equals *Falstaff* is Kurosawa's *Throne of Blood*. It is derived from *Macbeth* but even more removed from Shakespeare than is *Falstaff*, since it freely alters the characters and the plot and, more important, is in Japanese, making no attempt to use even a translation of Shakespeare's words. The avoidance of Shakespeare's words is an asset here, since it allows the camera to do what a camera should do. (An English-language version simply cannot jettison the text, except in such a scene as the battle in *Falstaff*. Even in Shakespeare's day the text of battle scenes must have been less impressive than some of the displays of swordsmanship.) *Throne of Blood* does not even seem to make a great deal of use of Japanese words: there are long silences when characters stare into space, communicating less with others than with themselves. Even more important, the misty forest is a character. The title of the film in Japanese is *Kumonosu-Jo*, the castle of the spiderweb: the wood is like a web that entangles its invaders. This forest-web, of course, is also an image of Washizu's (Macbeth's) mind, a maze in which he comes to destruction.

Like the use of Japanese instead of English, the Japanese landscape—not what we are used to—is also an asset to this film set in a remote past. As Welles, glancing at Olivier's *Henry V*, somewhat waspishly but shrewdly complained, historical films suddenly strike a false note when those quaintly costumed performers step out of their appropriately appointed dwellings and onto a battlefield. The reality of natural surroundings emphasizes the unreality of the actors. But in *Throne of Blood* the strange Japanese landscape, with its labyrinthine forest, seems to go with the costumes, at least to Western eyes. (The Japanese themselves apparently find it acceptable, too, because they are used to films showing medieval samurai like Washizu moving in the landscape. Such films are a national industry, like our westerns—whose cowboys *do* seem to go with the landscape.)

No more need be said here about *Throne of Blood* (other than to give it A), but its conspicuous success inclines one to think that the best cinematic versions of Shakespeare (like the best operatic versions) may come from non-English-speaking countries. This is to generalize from a single notable success, but what other generalizations can be offered? I can think of only one, and it is even more despairing. Some seventy years of experimentation with Shakespeare on film offers little to refute the argument of the police lieutenant who in 1908 wanted to censor a film version of *Macbeth* because of its gory stabbings. (Luckily, time took him before he could see Roman Polanski's *Macbeth* [1971], which shows the Thane of Cawdor's head roll from the block.) The lieutenant was writing in the days of the nickelodeon, so his reference to admission fees must be greatly altered, but the gist of his idea can stand: "Shakespeare is art, but it's not adapted altogether to the five-cent style of art."

Index